The Joshua Ministry

Keys to Becoming an Effective Associate Minister & Pastor

The Joshua Ministry

Keys to Becoming an Effective Associate Minister & Pastor

David W. Hopewell, Sr., D.Min.

The Joshua Ministry

Keys to Becoming
an Effective Associate Minister
& Pastor

David Hopewell, Sr., D. Min.

The Joshua Ministry Keys to Becoming an Effective Associate Minister & Pastor training manual is designed to equip the associate minister and foster unity between the associate minister and the pastor. It is also are source to help train others, enabling their improved understanding and appreciation of the roles and responsibilities in leading. While each church is autonomous, this manual provides overarching principles that apply effectively in all churches. You are invited to realize the full value of *The Joshua Ministry Keys to Becoming an Effective Associate Minister & Pastor* training manual through application.

Table of Contents

Are you

a

Servant Leader?

The History of the Joshua Ministry

The Joshua Ministry began in 1997 after I accepted a ministry position at Greenforest Community Baptist Church in Decatur Georgia, under the leadership of the late Dr. George O. McCalep, Jr. The evangelism strategy and principles we used were based on several chapters from the Book of Joshua. It is these scriptures which proved to be the basis for our approach to evangelism, including step-by-step principles for successfully 'possessing the land through evangelism. In 2001, the book, *The Joshua Ministry; God's Witnessing Army* was published. It featured the principles and strategies for evangelism based on unity. In reflecting on eight years and seven publications later, it is evident that the central element of my call and of my writings is to promote our working together. God has directed my steps and continues to develop me personally and the Joshua Ministry as well. In 2004, my book *Keys to Becoming an Effective Associate Minister & Church Leader*, was published. It promotes the development of associates and in emphasizes unity with their pastors.

In over thirty years of ministry, God has allowed me to serve as an associate to pastors specializing in church growth and evangelism. The twelve years I served as Minister of Evangelism at Greenforest Community Baptist Church were especially rewarding and provided tremendous experience.

I give God honor for allowing me to serve as consultant for the Atlanta Baptist Association. My role then was to help churches develop strategies for effective outreach to their communities.God has allowed me to serve on committees for the Southern Baptist Organization where I contributed to their strategies by developing "The Net," an Evangelism Strategy for the twenty-first century. It was also my privilege to work as a contract worker for The North American Mission Board.At that time I was a trainer and I also developed evangelism strategies for African-American churches.

I am currently an adjunct professor at Beulah Heights University in Atlanta, where I teach Urban Evangelism and Leadership.

My training, circumstances, events, experiences, and most of all the direction from the Lord has inspired me to launch The Joshua Ministry Inc., The Joshua Ministry School of Evangelism, and The Joshua Ministry School of Associate Minister Training.

My sincere prayer is that the biblical principles, personal experiences, and knowledge conveyed in this manual will aid your personal development and inspire you to be all God is calling you to be.

David W. Hopewell, Sr.D. Min.

How To Use This Manual

These twelve Instructor led group paced sessions may be presented in several ways. Choose the option below that best meets the needs of your congregation or group.

Option #1: Once a Week for Twelve Weeks

Sessions are structured for delivery in two hour increments. The presentation of class content alone will take approximately ninety minutes. Classes may be less than ninety minutes based on class participation.

Option #2: Weekend Modular

Sessions are held on non-consecutive weekends (Fridays and Saturdays). Sessions are two hours in duration. However, delivery may be condensed to 90 minutes.

Option #3: Weekends

Sessions are scheduled on two consecutive Fridays and Saturdays. Sessions are two hours in duration but may be condensed to ninety minutes.

Are you

a
Servant Leader?

What Pastors Desire from Their Associate

This session looks at leadership through the lens of the pastor, and will prepare the associate for subsequent lessons. It will also help broaden the student's understanding of leadership responsibilities.

As the Senior Pastor of your church, right now, what expectations would you have of your associates? Some associates feel they can do a better job than their current pastor but in actuality they may lack the experience. Most profoundly they may also lack the anointing of the pastorate. Some associates do not consider the passage of Scripture from Galatians 6:7 which points out that we will reap what we have sown. If we are not faithful in our current church, we should not expect others to be faithful in our ministry. If we do not tithe, support, work in the church, buy into the vision of the church—you fill in the blank—we should expect to reap this same lack of faith from our followers as we occupy the lead position.

Pastors primary expectations of associates are those things which should be common and normal between employer and employee. Though not limited to the following, these expectations include someone who is:

- Faithful
- Loyal
- Supportive (Supports the church with time, talent, and treasure)
- Trustworthy
- Disciplined in manners of their own life
- Spiritual
- Teachable
- Submissive to authority and is not in an abusive manner
- Committed to the vision
- Congenial (Has a good relationship among members of the church)

Let's take a moment now to identify and briefly discuss any additional traits, agreements or disagreements. Let's not make the pastor's job harder than it already is. Consider serving them as unto the Lord, Considering what we are sowing ourselves.

The pastor knows that the role of the associate minister is likely the most misunderstood role in today's church. In addition to being misunderstood, it is also surrounded with frustration, discouragement, and suspicion.

While other leadership roles are defined in bylaws or ministry descriptions, the associate minister's role seems less well defined. It seems to be based on assumption, demand or need. Some pastors use associate ministers as personal caretakers and are serving without any or limited spiritual training or a plan for spiritual growth.

Associate ministers are also often under suspicion by just being in ministry. God forbid that they might actually be able to teach, preach, or possess any type of spiritual gift. Their motives are subject to further scrutiny. Flowing from these suspicions are possible assumptions that "they think they can preach, or teach." Or, they are trying to take over the church. While this is often far from the truth, these assumptions leave associates frustrated, wounded and, sometimes discouraged. Restricted involvement and lack of development may cause associates to withdraw from service or seek greener pastures. While there are many ministry opportunities and corners from which to preach, I have found that not being used within the church is one of the main sources of frustration and discouragement to associate ministers. Another source of discouragement and frustration is waiting on "the call—the idea that one day they will have their own church or ministry, but not yet, not today.

The pastor knows that the associate minister is a leader. So, before we examine the role and function of the associate minister, we should examine leadership. Let's start by asking some general questions relative to church leadership.

Questions

Record your response to the following questions:

1. What is the current state of leadership in the church today?

_____

_____

_____

_____

2. Is there a lack of godly leadership in the body of Christ today?

_____

_____

_____

3. How would you recognize godly leadership?

_____

_____

_____

_____

_____

_____

4. What qualifies a person to be a leader?

_____

_____

_____

_____

_____

_____

5. What do you imagine yourself doing as a leader?

_____

_____

_____

_____

_____

_____

There are some real problems in church leadership today. If we live in sin, lean more on education and personal development than God, refuse to allow God to develop us spiritually, and live in hypocrisy, we will never be successful associate ministers and leaders.

While we all struggle daily to bring our bodies under subjection, we should not live in sin as a lifestyle. The body of Christ has been tainted by misuse of authority, personal kingdom building instead of building up God's kingdom, prejudice based on class and gender, and moral failure by our church leaders. All the while, God holds leadership to a higher set of standards than what has been demonstrated to both the church and the world. Again, we are all subject or prone to sin. But there is a difference between "falling short" through sin, and choosing to make sin one's lifestyle. When we use the office of ministry to sin or to support a sinful lifestyle, we have misused the office of leadership and misrepresented God's kingdom to the world .

Although talent, skills, and education are important, they cannot sufficiently nor successfully lead God's people to the promised land. Can you imagine Moses trying to lead people to the land of promise with only his skills and the education he received in Pharaoh's house? Leaders can never take people where they have never been. We will look at this principle in a subsequent lesson.

Spiritual development along with one's skills and education, is required to successfully led people to the "promised land." God has a process that He takes leaders through. He may use circumstances to draw an anointing upon us, to develop character, and bring us into a place of brokenness. He may even move us geographically. I have found God has a process that develops us spiritually and leads us to a place of dependency upon His Word. Apart from His processes we can only lead with our skills or our own intellectual capacity.

To live in hypocrisy is to convey something that we aren't. One false persona of leadership is that of perfection. Nothing could be further from the truth. We are not perfect, nor are we without sin. How can we expect to help others who struggle with their own truth of imperfection, if we refuse to show them our scars and wounds? Anointing comes out of the scars and wounds of our experience. God already knows our sin, so we might even ask, "Though we are prone to sin, do we confess our sin, or has it become a lifestyle?"

In Psalm 51, David talks about three categories of sin. He first mentions "transgression," which is a willful act committed by choice. He then mentions "iniquity," which is gross sin and is satanic in nature. Finally, he mentions "sin," which includes the idea of missing a target. When we chose to continue to sin as a lifestyle (when we stop trying to overcome our sin) we hinder others and remain unwilling to seek God's forgiveness.

Such a lifestyle without spiritual discipline conveys to others that living in sin is acceptable. My hope is for leaders, we realize that continuing to practice a sinful lifestyle leads to reckoning with God, which may take the form of brokenness over our sin. In Psalm 51, David came to a point of brokenness. It is only at the point of brokenness that we will put away our sin.

As we take this journey, expect to go where you have not gone before. Look for God in every lesson. God is going to invite and introduce you to a process that will shape, mold, and develop you. If you have prayed, "God use me," did you truly mean it? Will you truly submit to the process?

For those who seek position and the praise of others, God cannot trust or impart His anointing for the deliverance of others without your true spiritual development. However, for those who truly seek God as a deer pants after a water brook, you will find Him.

Psalm 103:7 states that the children of Israel knew His acts, but Moses knew His ways. Acts are what they perceived as He demonstrated His power to deliver them from Egypt. On the other hand, Moses knew His ways, the way and purpose with which God does things. When knowing the ways of God, we will be more prone to go through the process of spiritual and character development, experiencing power through and with God.

It is evident, based upon the lack of demonstrated character, that some leaders have refused to comply with the process. When we practice sin as a lifestyle and justify our sinful actions, we are rebelling against God's developmental processes.

The following topics will comprise our study for the next twelve weeks. Listen for God as He speaks to you. Pray and be willing to go through the process.

Session 2: This session examines different types of leadership styles.

Session 3: This session focuses on how God calls leaders.

Session 4: This session focuses on the associate minister's call, gifts, and personal development.

Session 5: This session focuses on how God spiritually prepares a leader through circumstances.

Session 6: This session is a continuation of the previous session.

Session 7: This session examines the calls of the associate minister.

Session 8: This lesson examines the role of the senior pastor, his specific functions, duties, and assumed roles.

Session 9: This session conveys reasons associates are called to their current church, and how and when to leave properly.

Session 10: This session focuses on ceremonies and functions of the church.

Session 11: This session seeks to challenge the associate minister to serve the pastor and church during times of conflict.

Session 12: This session seeks to help the associate minister understand weakness in leadership. Students will learn how to cover leaders during times of weakness.

Types of Leadership In The Church

Understanding leadership styles will aid in leadership development. In this lesson, we merely seek to introduce students to some of the different leadership styles. All leadership styles are not presented here; however, the manual does include basic information relative to the associate's role and function. The intent is to focus on the associate's spiritual development.

Familiarizing oneself with leadership styles can help you identify your own and other's style. For example, if your leader is very demanding or micromanages, learning his or her style will help you understand and lessen the strain on your relationship. We will begin our study with leadership styles and conclude with types of leaders in the church. We will give brief descriptions in this manual. Our focus is to give basic information, then concentrate more on the associate's relationship with his/her pastor, congregation, duties and spiritual development. We also hope that the information given will inspire students to engage in additional study. However, we encourage those who teach from this manual, to build upon the brief explanations. On-site campus lectures may include additional information.

Autocratic Leadership Style

Leaders whose dominant style is autocratic tend to exercise as much power and decision-making authority as possible. Such leaders tend to avoid consulting employees and resist their input. Those serving under this leadership style are simply expected to obey orders without variance or explanations. The weakness in this leadership style is that it results in high turnover and employee absenteeism.

Bureaucratic Leadership Style

Those whose leadership is predominantly bureaucratic tend to manage "by the book." Everything must be done by policy and procedure. If it is not done by the book, the leader refers to the next level above him or her. Those with this style enforce rules. There is no grace, only law.

Democratic Leadership Style

The democratic leader is one that participates and involves others in the decision making process. Successful outcomes or productivity is viewed by this leader as team results.

Laissez-faire Leadership Style

Leaders who utilize this style as their primary means of leading, provides little or no direction and allow as much freedom as necessary.

These descriptions of leadership styles were provides as a snapshot of the basic secular categories of leadership styles. At this time, I would like to provide a few additional descriptions of leadership styles, but this time from a biblical perspective.

Servant Leadership Style

Servant leadership sounds like an oxymoron (a term embodying two opposing concepts, a paradox). Some accepted examples: are: dark light, old news, deafening silence, bittersweet, virtual reality, and servant leader.

When we think of leadership today, we don't think of leaders doing menial tasks. We basically think of them as people giving instructions and being catered to. However, the biblical leader is to be a servant. In fact, Jesus explains , that the one who serves, is the greatest in the kingdom. (Luke 22:26). As leaders, we are to be servants. We are expected to not only lead, but to also serve humanity; hence, servant leadership. Our best example is the person of Jesus Christ.

We are told in Philippians 2 that Jesus made Himself nothing, taking on the very nature of a servant. This was Jesus, the Christ, the Son of God, the One from Heaven. If anything, He should have been the one served. Yet, we see Him serving others. He demonstrated serving in the lowest possible manner as an example to us all. In John 13, Jesus rose from supper, girded Himself with a towel, and washed the disciples' feet. How could He do that? The keys are found in verse 3. Jesus knew the Father had put all things in His power (authority). He was from God (born of God). Lastly, He was going back to God (his heavenly home).

When we come to the place that we know we have authority in God, that we are born of Him, and that our eternal state is in heaven, we can then take off our outer garments, those things that hinder us from serving, and pick up a towel and serve humanity. It is hard to do menial tasks when we think others will label us based on the task we perform. If you visited my church and saw me (a minister) cleaning the restroom, you might think I am the maintenance worker or custodian. We tend to define the "title" by the tasks we see being performed.

However, if you know you have authority, are born of God, and some day will live in heaven, the outward perception of the task does not define your title, identity, or even leadership function. Regardless of the task performed you are still who you are. Even if people labeled you from the outside, the inside will stand in its righteousness and declare who you really are, a child of God. If we serve, God will call us the greatest.

As leaders who represent the kingdom of God, we should live in a posture of service. God hates pride (Proverbs 6:17). The promise of being humble paves the way for exhortation (1 Peter 5:6).

Biblical Leaders

We will now look at leaders in the church and their functions. The New Testament reveals a variety of leaders in the church. The first five are part of what is known as the five-fold ministry gifts. They are: apostles, prophets, evangelists, pastors, and teachers (Ephesians 4:11). Their responsibility is to train the body of Christ until she becomes mature.

Apostles

The original meaning is "one who has been sent" an ambassador, or one who represents another. The term was used by Jesus when He explains that a "messenger" is not greater than the one who sends him (John 13:16). Apostles are mentioned in 2 Corinthians 8:23. The twelve disciples who were sent out by Jesus were called apostles (Mark 3:14). Paul and Barnabas were called apostles (Acts 14:4,14). Some false apostles are mentioned in 2 Corinthians 11:13 and Revelations 2:2. God appointed others to be apostles (1 Corinthians 12:28; Ephesians 4:11).

What role did the apostle have in the early church? The disciples and Apostle Paul were instrumental in beginning the church. Some qualifications are mentioned in Acts 1:21–25. Paul mentioned his qualifications in 1 Corinthians 9:1. The apostle is a preacher of the gospel who represents Christ.

Prophets

Prophets help the church by comforting, edifying, encouraging, instructing, strengthening and sometimes predicting. Paul listed prophecy as one of the gifts of the Holy Spirit (1 Corinthians 11:5). Being a prophet is a "spiritual gift" (1 Corinthians 14:37). Paul urged the Corinthians to desire the gift of prophecy (Corinthians 14:1,39); however, based on his use, it rarely means predicting the future. Paul explains, that everyone who prophesies speaks to men for their strengthening, encouragement and comfort, he who prophesies edifies the church. (1 Corinthians 14:3-4). Prophecy is also for instruction (1 Corinthians 14:31).

Evangelists

The word "evangelist" is only used three times in the New Testament. Philip was called an evangelist (Acts 21:8). Paul exhorted Timothy to "keep your head in all situations, endure hardness, do the work of an evangelist, and discharge all the duties of your ministry" (2 Timothy 4:5). In Ephesians 4:11, Paul says that God gives evangelists to the church. The evangelist has a gift to preach and lead others to Christ.

Pastors

The word "pastor" appears only once in the New Testament (Ephesians 4:11). The Greek word is usually translated "shepherd." Luke 2:8 uses the word in its literal meaning: "There were shepherds living out in the fields nearby, keeping watch over their flocks at night."

"Shepherd" is often used metaphorically for spiritual leadership. Jesus referenced Himself as a shepherd (John 10:11–14). In Matthew 9:36, people were like sheep without a shepherd. Paul exhorted Ephesian elders that the Holy Spirit had made them overseers of a flock. He exhorted them to shepherd the church (Acts 20:28). Peter also told elders to shepherd the flock, serving as overseers (1 Peter 5:2).

Teachers

Teachers play an important role in the church. A teacher is one that imparts information for the purpose of knowledge and/or skills transfer. Teachers build on the foundation of salvation to equip the saints. They impart doctrine, principles, and a general knowledge of Christendom.

Armor-bearer

The term armor-bearer appears eighteen times in the Old Testament. It is first mentioned in Judges 9:54 where Abimelech requested his armor-bearer to kill him so it would not be said that a woman killed him. The next place in Scripture is 1 Samuel 14:7, where Jonathan's armor-bearer is mentioned. In 1 Samuel 16:21, it says that David became Saul's armor-bearer. The next place in Scripture we see the term used is in 1 Samuel 31:4, where Saul requested to be killed by his armor-bearer. In 2 Samuel 23, David's mighty men are mentioned.

The original meaning is "to lift, advance, bear, bear up, carry away, cast, desire, furnish, further, give, help, hold up, lift, pardon, raise, regard, respect, stir up, or yield." The second Hebrew word means "to end, complete, consume, destroy utterly, be done, finish, fulfill, long, bring to pass, wholly reap, or make clean riddance.' From these two words we understand that the armor-bearer was to stand beside his leader to assist him, to lift him up, and to protect him against any enemy that might attack him. It also means to serve, help, in life, fight of faith, attend to, minister to, care for, help, be of use, assist, benefit, promote, support, make easy for, nourish, and encourage.

While biblical support exists for the armor-bearer, there has been misuse by some pastors. As leaders, we should be very careful how we care for and handle people. At no time should we misuse people to benefit our own agenda or as a point of pride.

Bishops

In many denominations, a bishop is a person who supervises all the churches in a region. There was more than one bishop in Ephesus and more than one in Philippi (Acts 20:28; Philippians 1:1). Paul sent for the elders near Ephesus, called them all bishops, and told them to be pastors of the church (Acts 20:28). In Philippi, Paul greeted the bishops and deacons without mentioning pastors or elders; possibly suggesting that bishop, pastor, and elder are similar terms. A bishop is an overseer, a leader, someone who watches over others (Acts 20:28). Look up these additional passages for your study: 1 Timothy 3, and Titus 1:7.

Elders

"Elder" is the most common translation of *presbyteros*, which means "older man." The word was used for the prodigal son's older brother (Luke 15:25). Revelations 4:4 is depicts elders in heaven. The word was used in the Christian community, too (Acts 11:30; 15:2). Peter and John called themselves elders (1 Peter 5:1; 2 John: 1; 3 John:1). Following are additional passages for your personal study: Acts 11:30, 15:2; 1 Timothy 5; Titus 1:5; James 5:14; and 1 Peter 5.

Deacons

The Greek word *diakonos* means "assistant, someone who helps others." The word is also used to denote an office in the church (Philippians 1:1; 1 Timothy 3:8–13). The seven men chosen in Acts 6:3 have often been understood as deacons because they served. The New Testament church had various leaders, who served members. Their service included physical service, administration of the Word of God, and managing functions of the church. We should always serve with the purpose to help others and bring glory to God.

Questions

1. What type of leadership style best describes you?

_____

_____

_____

2. What type of leadership style best describes your pastor?

_____

_____

_____

3. What type of leadership style challenges you most?

_____

_____

_____

4. Discuss the role of the armor-bearer today relative to use and misuse.

_____

_____

_____

5. How do you view ministry based on your gifts?

_____

_____

_____

_____

Notes

Are you

a
Servant Leader?

The Call to Leadership

My mind goes back to the movie, *"Sister Act"* starring Whoopi Goldberg. In one scene, she was asked, "When did you get the call?" The "call is a summons from God to serve in some form of ministry. Among the questions this raises are: What is the call? What is the purpose of the call? How many calls are there? How does God prepare someone for "the call?" We hope to shed some light on the questions as we negotiate aspects of this lesson. How God prepares us will be the subject of the next two lessons.

For years God has been developing me. Believe me, I am a work in progress. However, it was not until I was introduced to two books bearing the same title, *The Making of a Leader* by Frank Damazio and the other by Robert Clinton that I was able to articulate my experience. The same process God had been using to develop them, was the process He was using to develop me. I knew they could describe the process only through their personal experience. While each man experienced different circumstances and, at times, used different biblical text to explain the lessons they learned, their process and lessons yielded the same outcome. Their terms (process, principles, and patterns) have become part of my experience and vernacular as well. Both books caught my attention because as I read them, I found very few persons were able to articulate anything similar to what God had been doing in my life. I have come to refer to it as the process of God, or the spiritual development process. Based on the things they presented in their books, I know they have been where most of us have not gone.

The following three sections describe tests God takes us through to develop us spiritually. I had never placed them in any order as the authors had. Both authors presented timelines of development that I will reference in chapters four and five. I have taught on tests and have even mentioned a few of them in my associate minister book. Some of the tests the authors mention are the same; however, the experience, as well as some of the tests are different.

You can't take people where you have not been, nor can you use their armor, if you have not prove it. Remember David (1 Samuel 17:39). God has taken me through many experiences. I credit both authors for helping me put handles on what God has been doing in my life.

Definition

The word "call" has various definitions. However, we want to focus on one particular meaning of the word. I like the biblical thought of "seize," which gives us a picture of God laying hold on us, never forcefully, but by invitation. We will see this and additional components as we examine the call of Moses in this lesson.

Purpose of Calling

The purpose of a calling is three-fold. First, the call is an invitation to fulfill God's purpose. Secondly, the call is to serve others. Finally, the call is to bring glory to God.

The call is different from the assignment. The call is simply an invitation to respond to His voice or dealings. The assignment may be something totally different. Most times when we acknowledge "the call" our reference is to the pulpit or preaching. I propose the call is our acknowledgement of saying yes to His voice and dealings. Then He will continue to prepare us and reveal the assignment or mission. We will discuss this as we proceed through this section.

Three Calls to Leadership

Everyone in ministry has not been called by God! I hope that statement does not shock you. The following are ways leaders assume a leadership role, including being "called."

Self-Appointed Leadership

The title speaks for itself. When we are inspired by something other than God, and proceed with selfish motives to gratify our own ambition or desires, rather than fulfill God's purpose, bring glory to His name, promote His kingdom, or are not genuinely concerned about people and their plight, we have called ourselves. A sure way to recognize a self-appointed leader is by using the following check points.

- Do they reference themselves (I) or God?
- Do they promote God's work or their own?
- Do they point people to God or themselves?
- Are they genuinely concerned about others?
- Do they use the name of Jesus in conversations?

When we talk about self-appointed leadership, the examples of Dathan, Korah, and Abiran come to mind. Read Numbers 16 for the history.

Along with about two hundred fifty men, they rose up against Moses and his leadership. They were already in a position of leadership, but apparently desired the head position. Their complaint was that Moses had gone too far. Moses and Aaron were not the only ones in the group who were holy. They asked, "Why do you place yourself in leadership above the people?" Moses even went on to tell them that God had separated them and given them a special place in Him and in ministry. Moses continually tried to talk them out of their rebellion. Aaron even tried (to no avail) to make an atonement for them (Numbers 16:46). As a result, 14,700 people perished as they followed self-appointed leadership.

Man-Appointed Leadership

We will talk more about Man -appointed leadership later and examine the biblical character Joshua. However, this occurs when others become the overwhelming voice of God in our lives. Voices tempt us to proclaim ourselves as leaders or push us into positions without God's summons. Oh yes, we say God has called us. Yet, we have been deceived. An example of this is Saul (1 Samuel 8). God's desire was to make Israel a theocratic nation, God-ruled. However, the people wanted a king, not God. I know one may argue the point that God picked him; however, he was the people's choice, not God's. They wanted an appointee, and God consented. Here are a few observations that can help us identify man-appointed leadership:

- Division and wounded congregants are left behind in their quest to rule at the top.
- Rules and requirements are relaxed or totally disregarded to ensure their appointment.
- Manipulation occurs in the selection process.
- Education and personal achievements are of greater concern than spiritual character.
- The advice and feelings of others are disregarded in the selection process.
- Little prayer or biblical principles are used in the process, or they are used to cover the true motives or to manipulate others.
- There are people who will push, push, push, and push to ensure the selection.

God-Appointed Leadership

Those who are called by God, appointed by Him, anointed by Him, separated for His use, and sent by Him are examples. You can pick any one of the following biblical characters as God-appointed leaders: Abraham, Moses, Joshua, Jeremiah, Isaiah, and the list goes on. This would include believers who are called to the five-fold ministry office of apostle, prophet, evangelist, pastor, and teacher. Those who function in these offices, teach and train others until they come into unity and the fullness of Christ (Ephesians 4:11–14). All believers are called first to salvation and secondly to service.

God called Moses through a burning bush (Exodus 3:1–3). He called Samuel by an audible voice (1 Samuel 3:1–9). He may do that today. God does what He wants, and I will not limit Him. Let me also suggest additional ways God calls leaders:

- God calls us through His Word. This occurs when you read the Word or through the preached Word of God. You will feel as though God is speaking directly to you. The Word comes alive and seems to jump off the pages.
- God calls us by the Holy Spirit (Acts 13:2). While they fasted and prayed, "...*the Holy Spirit said, separate Paul and Barnabas for the work I have called them.*"
- God calls those in spiritual authority through His guidance (Deuteronomy 31:1–13; Acts 1:12–26).
- God calls us in dreams, as He did Joseph (Genesis 37:5).

The Call of Moses

Over the years, the character Moses has become one of my favorite and my focus of study. Moses spent forty years in Egypt, forty years in the desert, and forty years leading the people of God. His physical call came in the desert some eighty years after birth. The call of Moses came through a burning bush. The assignment, or what God wanted him to do, was given after he answered the call. The assignment, or what I call his spiritual DNA, was evident from his early days. We will discuss that later. His call in Exodus 3 reveals that God called him as he kept the sheep of his father-in-law. The encounter Moses had with the burning bush represents the Spirit of God that is calling within us.

"The spirit in man *is* the candle of the Lord, searching all the inward parts of the belly" (Proverbs 20:27). "But *there is* a spirit in man: and the inspiration of the Almighty giveth them understanding" (Job 32:8). These Scriptures teach that God speaks to the hidden man of the heart. So according to the Proverbs passage, when God speaks to us, He lights our candle. Inwardly, He inspires us according to the passage in Job. Most times we don't recognize His inspiration because it's a still small voice. Remember Elijah's experience (1 Kings 19: 9–18). Sometimes we disregard its prompting because we are so involved with our own agenda. Usually, when God lights our candle (our inner man) it's for us to pull aside and pray, which requires us to make a sacrifice. Moses had to turn aside, or relinquish what he was doing to respond to God's invitation (Exodus 3:4).

The call of God is always in direct response to what God has seen, heard, and knows (Exodus 3:7). God saw the afflictions of His people, He heard their sorrows, and He knew the burdens of their task masters. When He sees, hears, and knows the plight of a person or people, He extends an invitation to someone who has a passion in a specific area.

The question that could be asked is, why Moses? My response would be, why not Moses? Out of all the Hebrews in Egypt, Moses was the only one who had a passion for deliverance. In Exodus 2, he delivered one of his Hebrew brothers was about to be killed by an Egyptian (Exodus 2:12). The next day, he saw two Hebrews fighting and brought deliverance when he broke up their fight (Exodus 2:13). After leaving Egypt, he went to Midian where he interceded when the daughters of Jethro were being driven away from a water hole (Exodus 2:15–21). Moses was simply acting out what was within him, his spiritual DNA.

Moses never had a problem with what God was going to do until God said, "thou art the man!" We do all we can to prepare ourselves for "the call." We tell God and others, how we want God to use us. Yet, we may struggle when the assignment is revealed to us. We struggle when our call goes beyond the pulpit. We struggle when the voice and inspiration of God calls us into areas we fear. Then all the excuses begin.

In all his excuses, Moses missed what God said. *"I am come down to deliver them out of the hands of the Egyptians…" (Exodus 3:8). "…Certainly I will be with you and you will bring the people back to this place to worship me (Exodus 3:12)."* Moses continued giving God excuses and never heard God say, "I am going to do this, and not only that, but I am going to bring you back to this very place. In his fear Moses did not hear God say He would do the job, nor did he hear God promise to bring him back to His mountain.

When God calls us we can never pick the assignment. Sometimes we want the call, but don't want the assignment. I find the call is one thing, and the assignment is something different. The call is simply an invitation to be set aside for training, which we will discuss later. With the assignment comes the reality that you cannot do the job yourself and must depend upon God to succeed.

God takes our weakness and what is insignificant in our lives and turns it into ministry. The fear of the assignment caused Moses to ask, "Who am I that I should go unto Pharaoh?" (Exodus 3:11) I don't find that Moses had a problem speaking before this time. His inability and excuse prompted God to give him a spokesman, Aaron, his brother. Secondly, God asked him, "What's in your hand?" (Exodus 4:2). All the education and war training he possessed had been lost somewhere between Egypt and the desert. The only thing in his hand was a rod. Something that seemed so insignificant, yet in the hands of God, brought deliverance to a nation.

Several principles come from this. First, the most insignificant things are what God uses to bring deliverance in the lives of others. Secondly, when we pray and give what is in our hands back to God, it is like the five loaves and two fish that Jesus prayed over, disbursed, and gave to the crowd. Once given to Him and He blesses it, it becomes enough to meet the needs of the multitude. Thirdly, the things we struggle with will usually be the greatest areas of blessing in our lives. Fourthly, the very thing we fear may be tied to our assignment. Lastly behind the fear is the blessing.

We can never tell God where we won't go or what we won't do. The call, the training process, and the assignment all belong to Him. He calls us, prepares us, and gives us an assignment based on what He has seen, heard, and knows, and also on our passion and training. As long as we sit around waiting for an opportunity to preach or teach, or talking about the needs we see, but never responding the question can be asked, have we fulfilled our assignment? Maybe we have only answered the call, but not gone through the process or accepted the assignment.

Gifts of the Associate Minister

Every believer has at least one spiritual gift. It is important for associates and leaders to have a basic knowledge of gifts in the Bible. There are three sets of gifts mentioned in Scripture: Romans 12:6–8, 1 Corinthians 12:7–10, and Ephesians 4:11, totaling twenty-one gifts.

Motivational Gifts (Romans 12:6–8)

Seven of the twenty-one gifts, known as foundational or motivational gifts, are found in Romans 12. These gifts are given by the Father at birth and color everything we do from childhood to adulthood. They are:

- **Prophecy or perceiver -** as an adult, they perceive the will of God. As a child, they seem to be a tattletale. They are honest and see everything in black and white. This progresses into adulthood where there is no gray area with them. Their function is to help keep the body of Christ centered on God's Word.

- **Serving** - This is one who loves to serve others. They are "doers." As a child, they are the ones that play until they drop. As adults, they work until the job is finished without any regard for their own physical well-being. Servers think of how to meet others needs. They place others' needs and necessities above their own and thrive on the appreciation of others.
- **Teacher** - They love to study and teach truth. As children, they love reading. As an adult, they love facts and data.
- **Exhorter** - They encourage others, and love to make you feel better. As a child, they are the class clown. As an adult they love to give advice to others.
- **Giver** - They give time, talent, and money to benefit others. As a child they take good care of their toys and clothing. Some do not take their toys out of the wrapper. As adults, they give, but do not like to be recognized.
- **Administrator** - They organize. As a child, you would think they were lazy. At times, they give others assignments to accomplish a task that was assigned to them. As an adult, they can see who fits where in a project and do not care who gets the credit for a job well done. They just want the project to be completed.
- **Mercy** - They show mercy and compassion to others in need. As children, they tend to cry about things. As adults, they are easily hurt in relationships and by things not related to them. They feel the pain of others.

These descriptions are brief, but will give you some working knowledge so you can identify those working around you.

Five-Fold Ministry Gifts

There are five ministry gifts given by Jesus (Ephesians 4:11–13):
- **Apostle-** One who establishes and strengthens churches
- **Prophet-** One who speaks God's Word
- **Evangelist-** One who shares the gospel and teaches others to do so
- **Pastor-** One who shepherds God's people and has the ability to deal with the day-to-day.
- **Teacher-** One who instructs others in God's Word.

Spiritual Gifts

There are nine gifts given by the Holy Spirit. Three gifts reveal something. Three gifts say something, and three do something (1 Corinthians 12:7–10).

- **Word of knowledge -** Something known about someone that could not be known but through God.
- **Word of Wisdom -** Wisdom given by the Holy Spirit that enables a person to know what to do or say in any situation.
- **Faith -** Supernatural faith to believe God in any situation. There is also a measure of faith at salvation and the fruit of faith which is developed as we grow in our faith.
- **Gifts of healing -** Supernatural healing beyond natural means. Healing is usually gradual but not when supernatural healing takes place.
- **Working of miracles -** The power of God working beyond the natural laws. For example, a miracle would not be a foot being healed but a foot that grows or appears where one was lost.
- **Prophecy -** Proclamation from the Holy Spirit through an individual to encourage, exhorts, comfort, correct, or warn others. Sometime it is the proclamation of interpretation of tongues.
- **Discerning of spirits -** The ability to perceive what type of spirit, good or evil, that is in operation in a given situation.
- **Various kinds of tongues -** Languages given to the believer by the Holy Spirit.
- **Interpretation of tongues -** Supernatural ability to translate spoken tongue(s)

Associate's Introspection

As you reflect on the content of this lesson, take a moment to record what you believe God is saying to you.

1. What is God saying to you based on the content of this lesson?

_____

_____

_____

_____

_____

_____

_____

_____

_____

2. Are you called by God, people, or yourself?

_____

_____

_____

_____

_____

_____

_____

_____

3. Are you running from God's call or assignment? Are you making excuses?

_____

_____

_____

_____

_____

_____

_____

_____

Course of Action

After asking God's forgiveness, what course of action will you take to prevent the same occurrence? If you wish, use the space below to reflect and pen your course of action.

How God Prepares Leaders (Part 1)

The Lord is more concerned about our inward spiritual growth than the demonstration of our spiritual gifts. While most of us spend long hours and much money developing our cognitive knowledge and talents, we sometimes neglect the inner qualities from which true ministry flows. Education and the development of talents are very important; yet, there is training that goes beyond the cognitive and talent we aspire to develop, to spiritually prepare us for our ministry assignment.

Can you imagine Moses leading the Hebrews to the mountain of God or the promised land with only the education of Egypt? In fact, I don't see where he used anything he learned in Egypt during the process of deliverance. When he stood before God, he did not give God a bio with all the education and military training he received while in Egypt. Everything He learned in Egypt took a backseat to the spiritual weapons and process of God.

Without the process of God, we place our dependence upon our education or natural abilities. Not that we shouldn't use our natural abilities, but they can never produce the spiritual depth or experience needed to take God's people where He intends them to go, the promised land. A leader can never take a person where he or she has not been. If you are only educated by what has been naturally learned or your own abilities, it may limit your ability to fully lead people where God intends to take them spiritually.

The spiritual development process of God prepares leaders for their ministry assignment. If Moses had not gone through the process of the wilderness, he would not have had the spiritual insight or development to lead God's people. The education he received in Egypt was the best that could be had, but it was still not enough to lead people spiritually. His spiritual education came from God on the backside of the desert and through day-by-day experiences.

Perhaps we don't go through the process, or we resist the process because we don't interpret our circumstances and pain as the very instruments God uses to develop us. Within this state of spiritual atrophy, our knowledge of God can only be second or even third-hand—based on what we have only heard, but not yet experienced.

Psalms 103:7 tells us that the children of Israel knew God's acts, but Moses knew His ways. Our lack of understanding of God's ways limits our spiritual growth and our ability to lead others through their wilderness of life. We accumulate natural knowledge, develop our skills, earn degrees and proudly place certificates on our walls. That is all about us, but the process of God will develop us spiritually and leave us with an impediment, something that reminds us of our experience, humbles us, and creates a dependency upon God. This is all about Him. Without the visible scar, which is surface, or wounds, we will lean on our education or our natural abilities. These will not produce spiritual power or authority.

Paul said that he had come to a place of understanding. He understood that circumstances in life only positioned him to experience a state of weakness that the power of God might rest upon him (2 Corinthians 12:7–10).

Through the process of God, He develops us, cleanses us, and changes us into the image of Christ. God uses our circumstances and our wilderness experiences in our spiritual preparation. The wilderness is a place where God has chosen to humble us, to prove us, and to determine what is in our hearts—whether we will keep His commandments.

Tests are intended to bring us to the place where we fully understand, not cognitively, but experientially, "That man does not live by bread alone, but by every word that proceeds out of God's mouth" (Deuteronomy 8:3). God also uses circumstances to accomplish four key things in our lives. First, He uses circumstances to shift us geographically. Secondly, He uses circumstances to place an anointing on us. What we go through deepens us and produces power in us for the deliverance of others. Thirdly, He uses circumstances to build our character. Finally, He uses circumstances to bring us to a point of brokenness.

There are several tests God takes us through to develop us spiritually. The training process is different for each individual depending on his or her assignment. God proves or tests us (Genesis 22:1). God does not tempt us (James 1:13).

According to Mark 4:15, Satan is the tempter. There are five areas Satan uses to tempt us or cause the Word of God to be non-productive in our lives. When the Word is sown, Satan comes and uses affliction, persecution, cares of this life, deceitfulness of riches, and lust of that which is forbidden to uproot the Word from our lives (Mark 4:13–20).

The spiritual development process occurs over the course of our lives. Robert Clinton in his book, *The Making of a Leader*, lists six phases of development: (1) sovereign foundations; (2) inner-life; (3) ministering maturing; (4) life maturing; (5) convergence; and (6) afterglow. He mentions things that occur in each phase but also says some areas of development occur through the entire process, such as character.

Inner development occurs during the first three stages. During this time, most leaders become frustrated because they are looking for outward fruit in their ministry. However, the first three stages of development focus on inward growth, not outward growth. Ministry fruit manifests during phase three and beyond. Beyond phase three, tests occur through ministry challenges and tasks. I recommend his book; He can better explain the different effects that occur in each phase. I just know I was and am in a process of development. We have looked at the test of accepting our call and ministry assignment as we looked at the developing process of Moses. Now let's look at some tests that God takes us through to develop us spiritually.

Heart Test

The purpose of this test is to reveal what is sitting on the throne of our hearts in the place that is reserved for God only. The test challenges us to dethrone the things in our heart that we hold dear and place them before God.

Abraham was challenged with this test in Genesis 22. The first Scripture of this chapter opens with these words, "God did tempt Abraham." When we are tested, we are tested in three areas. According to 1 John 2:16, all that is in the world is the lust of the flesh, the lust of the eye, and the pride of life. The test of our heart exposes our love for something over our love for God.

Perhaps Abraham's test of the lust of his flesh came when he left home on his journey of faith. He may have been tempted to stay because of the security he had among family (Genesis 12). Perhaps the lust of the eye occurred when he saw the plains of Jordan but allowed Lot to choose the best part (Genesis 13:5–13). However, the test of the pride of life is found in Genesis 22.

Abraham prayed twenty-five years earlier for a son. To have a son brought pride to a Jewish family. Isaac represented his pride, and God was testing him to see if his love for Isaac was greater than his love for Him. Would he be willing to dethrone Isaac, if he indeed was on the throne of his heart? God could have said, "Go to Mount Moriah and offer up Isaac." However, He said, "Take now thy son, thy only son, Isaac, whom you love (Genesis 22:2)." Only son meant Isaac not Ishmael. God then emphasized Abraham's love for his son, possibly challenging him in this area.

Whatever the reason, Abraham put God first over his love for his family and possessions. He offered his son, his pride. The interesting part of the story is God's desire to know if Abraham was willing to sacrifice his only son for Him. Abraham did not have to commit the act, kill Isaac; he just had to be willing to offer him. Some things God tells us to dethrone are not good for us, so we need to discard them. Others things, as long as we are willing to dethrone them as Abraham did, God will give them back to us. He just wants to be first over family, friends, vocation, and passions.

Abraham did not stagger at what God had promised (Romans 4:20). This suggests he did not struggle placing God first, even if it meant the death of his son. Most of us struggle when it comes to releasing our kids to God. Don't let someone threaten or hurt one of our kids. In such a case, we won't need God to handle it, we will! I cannot, nor do I ever want to, experience the pain of losing a child. I have relatives and friends who have lost a child. What pain! I cannot take you where I have not been, but I believe I know what God desires from us. God wants us to live by his Word and praise Him in all things (Deuteronomy 8:3, 1 Thessalonians 5:18).

Time Test

Abraham was promised a son (Genesis 15:4). However, the actual time of Isaac's birth was twenty-five years later. The time test is designed to see if we will wait on God, or create an Ishmael—a son, but not the one God promised. Sometimes our inability to wait on God's timing tempts us to work things out on our own, or go to others to seek deliverance. They feel compassion for us, help us, and we testify how God delivered us. However, we may be placing a bandage on a cancer, settling for a short-term solution that was not God's best.

It is difficult to wait when you have the ability to make things happen or have contacts. Making things happen or using your contacts is not a bad thing, if God releases you to do so. I am not saying we do not need to fulfill our part. If you need a job, pray, and believe God, but ready your skills , and then go put an application in somewhere. We are to acknowledge Him in all our ways, and He will direct us (Proverbs 3:6).

Word Test

This test challenges us to not only wait on God, but believe His Word. The test produces a dependency upon God and establishes an absolute assurance that God's Word does work in any situation. The Scriptures we looked at relative to Abraham apply here too.

Sometimes the Word test comes to give experience to what we have been preaching. The one teaching or preaching the Word must be first partaker of what he or she preaches (2 Timothy 2:6). Some preach but have never experienced what they are preaching. When our experience matches our preaching, then we will preach with anointing and power. Additional Scriptures for the Word test will be examined later.

Character Test

This test reveals patterns of sin in our lives. God allows us to be in places and situations that test our character. Character is the person you really are behind closed doors. Some of us act one way when we are in public, but at home, we become someone different. Challenges are in the areas of the lust of the flesh, the lust of the eye, and the pride of life. Some of us have no problems in the area of what we call "big sins;" however, what about the little areas? Have you ever gone into a grocery store and selected a large amount of grapes, possibly costing $5.00, but when you got to the counter, they totaled $1.50. Would your character prompt you to be honest? Bad character would keep you silent, and you would be guilty of stealing! We steal time on our jobs, pick up items that don't belong to us, cheat, and then say God has blessed us.

Wilderness Test

As I shared earlier, the wilderness test proves what is in our hearts, whether we will serve God or not (Deuteronomy 8). The three primary areas of testing produce a dependency on God to fight our battles, heal us, and provide for our needs.

In Exodus 13, God led the children of Israel to the wilderness of the Red Sea. He purposely led them to a place where they were hedged in. The sea was in front of them, Pharaoh was behind them, and the mountains were on either side. God was teaching them that He would fight their battles, a lesson they did not learn. I will discuss this later.

The second wilderness God led the children of Israel to was the Wilderness of Shur (Exodus 15:22). They could not drink the waters because they were bitter. The purpose of the lesson was to teach them God was their healer. After this, God led them to a place called Elim. Elim was a place of palm trees, a place of refreshing. Elim taught them that even though there will be times of testing, God would, in the midst of testing, give times of refreshing. God is not interested in killing us, but developing us. His purpose is always redemptive in nature.

The third wilderness He led the Israelites to was the Wilderness of Sin (Exodus 16:1). It was here the children of Israel experienced hunger. Here, God was teaching that He would be their provider. When we do not pass the test, we will continue being tested until we do. However, the test will be more difficult the next time.

In Deuteronomy 1, Moses reiterates to a new generation what occurred forty years earlier. The number forty represents testing or trials. Their parents had left Egypt and journeyed to the mountain of God to receive God's moral and spiritual laws. They encamped there one year before leaving for Canaan. They were eleven days from the mountain of God, Kadesh-barnea. The number eleven represents imperfection. The number twelve represents governmental authority or rule. Had they continued their journey one more day or continued for twelve days, they would have entered Canaan (the promised land), which means they would have entered into authority and governmental rule with God. Going only eleven days, they remained in a state of imperfection.

There are five reasons the Israelites failed to enter the "promised land: 1. They rebelled (Deuteronomy 1:26); 2. They murmured in their tents (Deuteronomy 1:27); 3. Their brothers discouraged their hearts (Deuteronomy 1:28); 4. They had limited vision (Deuteronomy 1: 28); and 5. They just did not believe (Deuteronomy 1:32). After these occurrences, they chose to believe God, but it was too late. After they realized it was God, they proceeded to move out. They should have moved out when God told them, wholly following the Lord which would have demonstrated their faith. When they decided to move out, God was not backing them, and a great number were killed.

The interesting thing was after the event, God told Moses to take the children of Israel back to the Wilderness of the Red Sea (Deteronomy1:40). They had already been here, so why go back? The reason is they had not learned that He would fight for them. If you wonder why you continue to go through the same things over and over again, it may mean you have not passed the test.

If God will fight for us, heal us, and provide for us, what else do we need? These lessons prepare us to enter into the land ministry or whatever that God has promised us. If we don't learn the lessons we will not be prepared to function victoriously in the place God has promised us, or lead people through places we have not gone. Our failure to pass the tests in these areas will keep us wandering in the wilderness.

Associate's Introspection

Reflect on the tests described in this lesson and then answer the following questions.

1. What is God saying to you?

_____

_____

_____

_____

2. What is your response?

_____

_____

_____

_____

How God Prepares Leaders (Part 2)

A s we continue from last week, we will examine additional lessons we learn during times of testing.

Servant Test

This test reveals our ministry motives. If we are not preaching or teaching, will we continue to serve? My first perception of leadership was one where the leader received all the attention. I noticed the pastor being waited on—food was brought to him while he sat at the head table, doors were opened for him, and his brief case was carried. There is nothing wrong with these services in themselves. However, the perception leaves inspiring associates with the impression that this is ministry, being served not serving. They aspire to be in the pastoral role to be served, not to serve others.

Are we teaching associates how to serve hurting humanity? Are we teaching them how to model Jesus, pick up the towel, and minister to the least part of humanity? Jesus modeled the servant leader principle for us in John 13. He was from heaven. He came from a place where the streets are made of gold. He was King! If anything, the disciples should have washed His feet. How was He able to perform the most menial task? I believe the answer lies in John 13:3,. *"Jesus knowing that the Father had given all things into his hands, and that he was come from God, and went to God."*

This verse tells us how Jesus knew God had given Him authority. He knew he came from God (born of God) and that He was returning to God. Likewise, if we know we have authority in God, that we are born of Him (salvation), and that we are going to God (eternal life), then we can put on the towel of service and serve others.

Society conveys the message that if I clean a restroom, I must be a custodian. We associate the title with the task. If we know we have authority, are born of God, and have eternal life, the menial tasks we perform will not define who we are because we know. If I preach, teach, open a door for someone, or clean a restroom, I am still who I am— a man of God not a title. The title does not define who I am, but the task I performed reveals the heart of a servant.

Isolation Test

This test occurs when God shifts us geographically or gives us a ministry assignment. Elijah, the prophet, experienced this as he ran from Jezebel (1Kings 19). Sure signs of isolation are when you feel alone; you withdraw from those close to you; you don't want to talk on the phone; people and things aggravate you; you isolate yourself from others or you feel that you are afraid to live, but afraid to die. During times of isolation in my life, I have experienced all of the above. At the end of the experience, God shifted me in another direction and gave me a ministry assignment. Actually, I have stories and testimonies for each phase of testing.

In 1 Kings 19, Elijah was in a state of isolation running from Jezebel. He was in a cave when a storm, an earthquake, and a fire came. The storm speaks of our circumstances. During our circumstances we speak God's Word, we believe God, we pray, we work through things and so on. However, then comes the earthquake. The earthquake is what shakes your very foundation. Everything you believe is challenged, everything falls apart, and everything is shaken.

When my foundation was shaken, I experienced feelings I had never felt before, even suicidal. I experienced all the things I mentioned above, and everything I believed about God was challenged. I felt weak and vulnerable. Temptations were magnified, and I wanted to accuse God falsely.

Like Elijah, God spoke to me and said, "What are you doing down there?" He was not beating up on me. His voice was like an ocean full of butter. He said, "Look at you. You are just as valuable as anyone else." I was carrying an attitude that I am God's man and nothing can happen to me. Yet, I was feeling all the above. He never talked about the thing that placed me in my current state, but He did two things. First, He gave me a ministry assignment and secondly, He energized my inner man, my spirit. I felt His power charging me like a battery being charged. I have not been the same since. I thought, "Why couldn't He have just told me without the period of isolation? Sometimes God works through our experiences in such a way that He gets our full attention so when He speaks, we're pliable, ready, and listening.

Test of Opportunity

This test reveals inward motives and seeks to bring us to a place where we learn to wait on God to open doors of opportunity. When others are used or recognized instead of us, our true motives are revealed. Do we continue to walk in peace and wait on God to open doors and provide promotions?

I remember times when I was anxious to preach. In fact, I remember hurrying my family back to night service because the pastor allowed associates to preach during Sunday evening service. I thought if I returned before other associates, I would be chosen to preach.

God desires to bring us to a place where we are not anxious to preach. If we are anxious we are not ready. When we come to a place where we don't feel we are ready to be used or that we don't have anything to say, then we are ready. At this point, you have decreased, He has increased and doors will open. Remember, your gift will open doors for you (Proverbs 18:16).

Misunderstanding and Conflict Test

This test occurs to strengthen our personal use of the fruit of the Spirit. Experiences will test our response to others when we are misunderstood or conflict arises. Will we maintain Christian character during times of misunderstanding and conflict or respond like the world? Will we shut our mouths or give someone a piece of our minds?

This is not easy because the propensity to defend ourselves or clarify our motives when misunderstood is human nature. I am not saying we should never defend ourselves or clear up misunderstandings. God tests us and He does not want our help or our response.

I have found that when I do not have peace about saying something, or feel the need to defend myself, God will have someone else say what I was going to say or defend my cause. When I have peace, it is then that God will allow me to speak or defend myself. The important lesson is to obey the prompting or peace of God which will release you or restrain you.

A good Scripture to remember is Colossians 3:15, "And let the peace of God rule in your hearts…" This means let peace be an umpire. If the peace of God leaves, God is saying you are out at home plate. If you have peace about doing something, He is saying you are safe. Remember, if He does allow you to speak, it's not just what you say, but how you say it that matters. As leaders, we are held to a higher standard than those we lead.

Sometimes it is not time to speak. Sometimes God tests us to see if He can trust us. God reveals hidden things to His servants (Amos 3:7). Those He calls friends are privileged to know what He is doing (John 15:15). Some things God reveals He does not want disclosed or the fullness of time has not yet come to speak them. Some things are just intimate between you and God. The test must be learned because later on in times of ministry, God may want you to say something, not say something, or speak a specific word to a specific group of people or person. If you do not practice the presence of God and the prompting of His Spirit now, you will miss or question His direction later.

Warfare Test

Warfare is part of the Christian life. Sometimes I think some of the warfare we attribute to the devil is actually circumstances we have manufactured ourselves. For example, if I went outside in the dead of winter without a coat got sick, then solicited prayer for healing; because I was under attack from the devil, I would be wrong. The sickness was not demonic, but a result of my not being properly dressed for the weather conditions.

Yet, there are real attacks from a real foe. They come to cause us to doubt God or move us off focus. The attacks can be against your physical body, family members, finances, or mind. They can be acted out by people and can also be verbal in nature. In addition, my experience has been that when warfare occurs, it comes from unexpected places, places I thought were secure.

I have also experienced attacks coming from those closest to me. It's like Joseph and his brothers, a David and Absalom, David and Saul, Judas and Jesus. It is those closest to you. It's an inside kiss you have to watch out for. Attacks also occur against your physical body that cannot be explained by medical science. In fact, you may go to an emergency room and nothing can be found physically wrong with you.

The parable of the sower (Mark 4:14–20) gives us a view into Satan's purpose and areas in which he launches warfare. When the Word is sown, which could be by a preacher, someone giving you a word, or during your personal devotional time, Satan comes immediately to take away the Word sown into our hearts. He uses affliction, persecution, the cares of this life, deceitfulness of riches, and lust for that which is forbidden to lure us away from our stand on the principles of Scripture. These are the areas he uses as points of entry. These temptations come in three areas: lust of the flesh, lust of the eye, and the pride of life (Luke 4).

Authority Test

I believe this test produces the power of God for deliverance. The premise of this test goes back to Abraham in Genesis 22. I want to expand our study to include Luke 4 and 1 John 2:16.

The three areas we discussed above and the areas in which Abraham was tested are mentioned in 1 John 2:16 and Luke 4—lust of the flesh, eye, and pride. In Luke 4, Jesus was in the wilderness being tempted by Satan. The order of the tests was changed. When Jesus was tested, they came lust of the flesh, pride of life, and lust of the eye.

Luke 4 opens by telling us that "Jesus was full of the Spirit." However, after being tempted in all three areas, verse 14 tells us that He returned in the power of the Spirit. When Abraham passed the three tests, he received a natural blessing.

Could it be that we have been limited in the use of God's power to produce delivering power because we have something in our hearts, in the areas of lust of the flesh, lust of the eye, or pride of life that we esteem above God's Word?

Submission Test

This test is designed to see if we will submit to spiritual authority and to each other. Some have no problem submitting to their pastor but have a problem submitting to others in an authoritative role or to their spouses at home.

How do we respond to others when given instructions? Some say, they will not respond to anyone other than God. What is not understood is that the pastor is as God's representative. We have no problem acknowledging the pastor as the voice of God when preaching, but sometime we do when given advice or instructions.

Convergence

This is where it all comes together. Everything you have gone through comes to this season of time. God uses circumstances to build character, place an anointing on us, move us geographically, and to bring us to a point of brokenness. At the completion of the process we are broken, stripped, and feel like we have nothing God can use. However, it is the fullness of time the time for which you and I have been waiting. The time for God's purpose and ministry to go forward has come. The very thing you and I were created for stands before us. The world is waiting for us to accept the assignment and bring deliverance that has been long desired.

The story of Joseph illustrates this point. We are first introduced to Joseph in Genesis 37. Joseph was living with his father, Jacob, in the land of Canaan. God's ultimate purpose for Joseph was to guarantee the survival of a nation, thus protecting the seed and covenant through which the Messiah would come. At the same time, however, circumstances in his life came to destroy Joseph, the seed, and the covenant. He had a calling on his life, but why all the difficult circumstances? The first circumstance came from within his own family: an attempt to destroy the very one that God would use to save the Hebrew nation.

According to chapter 37 of Genesis, Joseph's brothers hated him and could not speak peaceably to him. They hated him because of his father's favoritism toward him, and because of the dreams Joseph had of his brothers bowing down to him. According to verse 37, they conspired to slay him. They stripped him of the coat, given to him by his father and left him for dead. However, even in all of this, God preserved Joseph by touching the heart of his brother Reuben, who suggested they not kill him, but place him in a pit. Once again, God sent a deliverer to preserve Joseph's life. This time the deliverer was in the person of his brother, Judah, who suggested that they not place him into a pit, but sell him. Joseph was sold to a band of Midianite merchants who took him to Egypt. However, this was all in God's plan. God knew that a famine would come some twenty years later. His plan was to preserve Joseph's family, thereby protecting the covenant God made to Abraham.

In Genesis 39, we find Joseph in Egypt. The second verse is a key statement: *"And the Lord was with Joseph, and he was a prosperous man…"* The favor of God introduced in this verse alerts us to the favor Joseph had on his life in the middle of his circumstances. In verses 3–6, it speaks again of this favor. Joseph's master saw that God was with him, and he found grace in his sight. The Lord made all that Joseph put his hands on prosper. The Egyptians were blessed because of Joseph.

God used the favor on Joseph's life to move him into a place of authority. In his new position, God, by His providential hands, used Joseph to save his family. However, the successes were short-lived. Potiphar's wife accused Joseph of a crime, of which he was not guilty. This was, once again, an attempt to foil God's plan and destroy His chosen people. Joseph was then placed in prison where circumstances and God's favor again put him in a position of authority. Two men needed to know the interpretation of their dreams. This was key because two years later, in chapter 41, Pharaoh would have a dream which would need an interpretation too. The chief butler remembered Joseph, who had interpreted his dream two years before. Once again, an attempt to foil God's plan to save a nation failed. God used favor to move Joseph, even in prison, to a position of authority, which placed him before the baker and butler, and ultimately before Pharaoh. God allowed Joseph to interpret Pharaoh's dream. This earned him a promotion from prison to second in command in Egypt, and placed Joseph, once again, in a position to save his nation. God even used the content of the dream to show Pharaoh that Joseph had the plan to save his people from the famine that would come. Again God preserved the seed and blessed others because of his people.

Chapters 42—50 give the account of Joseph's brothers coming to Egypt to buy corn because of the famine. God used the famine to cause His people to go to Egypt. Joseph had a new life and forgot about the vision of God. This is seen in the names of his two sons. *Manasseh* means, "God has made me forget my father's house," and *Ephraim* means "God has caused me to be fruitful in the land of my affliction." It was not until his brothers came to Egypt that

Joseph remembered the vision. Joseph revealed his identity to them in chapter 45 and told them that God had sent him before them to preserve their lives.

The circumstances in Joseph's life occurred for a reason. The stripping of the coat prepared him for the stripping of rank. The pit prepared him for prison." Joseph wanted the butler to defend him before Pharaoh. However, he was not broken yet. Chapter 41 opens by explaining what happened two years later, after the butler and baker were released from prison. Two years later, Joseph was now broken. During that time, no one vindicated him, no one remembered him, heaven was silent, and the vision or ministry seemed dead. He stood before Pharaoh and never opened his mouth to defend himself. He is broken now and could be used and trusted to carry out God's assignment.

Joseph had a problem with relationships. His brothers hated him and did bad things to him. His father rebuked him. Potiphar's wife lied on him, and the butler and baker did not remember him. Two years later, he was now broken. He had a problem with the very people God wanted him to deliver, and possibly would not have preserved life. God was developing Joseph and moving him into a position to save a nation. This was Joseph's assignment; however, it did not come without preparation and cost. It is clear that God chose Joseph to be the instrument He would use to preserve His seed and covenant. Although there were several attempts to foil God's plan, God used each attempt to move Joseph to a position of savior for a nation that would have otherwise been destroyed. God promoted Joseph in His timing. Only once did Joseph try to move beyond God's timing—when he told the butler and baker to remember him when they came before Pharaoh. However, it was not yet time for Joseph to be released from his circumstances. God was still working on him.

Sometimes we want to move beyond our circumstances or wilderness experiences, even though God's plan has not been completed. What if Joseph was not willing to forgive his brothers for their past treatment of him? This would have resulted in the destruction of a nation. If we have unrighteous things in our heart,, they can effect our ministry, also. What would you do if God told you to pray for the pastor you are trying so hard to get away from? God had to get all the junk out of Joseph's heart, or he may not have responded to his brothers in a favorable manner. All things came together at the fullness of time. The experiences, circumstances, gifts, and shifting all came so Joseph might be in a position to save a nation.

Associate's Introspection

1. As you reflect on the content of this lesson, where does God currently have you?

_____

_____

_____

_____

_____

_____

2. What lessons have you learned from the test you are currently going through?

_____

_____

_____

_____

_____

_____

_____

3. In addition to the tests listed in the previous lessons, what other test have you experienced and what lessons have you learned?

_____

_____

_____

_____

_____

_____

_____

The Role of the Associate Minister

Webster's Dictionary defines an associate as one who joins someone as a partner, or companion. It means to come into relationship for a cause. The role of associate ministers is one of support. Their duties should include their ministry assignments, which will vary based on the church or ministry, and all other assignments given by leadership. This definition takes me to Paul's writings found in 1 Corinthians 12, where he uses the analogy of the human body to represent the body of Christ. We are all called to a specific part of the body, with a specific function. Everyone can't be the head. We must be the part of the body God has chosen for us. Scripture teaches that all of us serve as different parts; however, most associates aspire to be the head (pastor).

Everyone is not called to be a head or pastor. Some are called to serve as pastor. Some, however, are called to serve others and be faithful in the role of support as Uriah was to King David (2 Samuel 11). Uriah was so faithful that he could not bring himself to go home during a time of war. I am not suggesting that we neglect home, but I am suggesting that our dedication and faithfulness to our pastor and the vision of the church be as Uriah's—faithful. Our dedication to God and family should come before our dedication to church. I will discuss this concept later.

Everyone is not called to have his or her own church or ministry. Someone has to be called to bring about another person's vision. I have visited cities throughout the country where there are literally churches on almost every corner. Has God really called all these men and women to pastor? While some of these churches were started by well-meaning pastors and associate ministers, some left their churches for the wrong reasons or in the wrong season. This is not to say that God will not call some associates to pastor at some point. However, some have not been called into the life of the pastorate at this point in time. They misjudged God's timing. Some left the church where they were serving with the wrong attitude. Associates have left in anger and continued to hold things in their heart against the pastor and ministry. There is a lot of backbiting and talk about pastors and ministries. If this fits you as an associate, you need to repent because you have put yourself in a very dangerous position with God.

There are also associates who left unprepared. They have not gone through their season of preparation. Some associates express what they experienced at their churches. Yet, their experiences are only a portion of the process God uses to develop them spiritually. As a result, they are not equipped and cannot effectively minister to others. The biblical pattern is clear; there is always a time of preparation.

After Jesus chose His disciples, they all went through a period of preparation. None of the disciples started out with their own ministry, but learned from the Master. They learned from Jesus before they were sent out.

Some associate ministers start off well. Usually before becoming an associate, they communicate to the pastor and congregation (oftentimes in testimony services) how God led them to that particular church. They even go as far as saying how faithful they will be, but as soon as they get a little authority, learn a few things, or receive a little responsibility, they get an itch to preach, or get a revelation on a Scripture, and feel it is time to move on. Some associates feel that God has called them to start their own churches. If our reasons for leaving are wrong, is God truly saying, "Move on"? Things have to be right on your part before God will release you to move on. Before leaving there must be confirmation by spiritual authority, and consideration must be given to when, where, and how. I will expound on these points in a later chapter.

Please understand that I am not saying that an associate, under these conditions, is not called. I am saying that, at some point, you have to make sure things are right before you move on. I know what it feels like to sit in a pew and think, "I am not being used." There are associate ministers who are very gifted, have a call and vision from God; are anxious and filled with zeal; and yet, are still sitting. Some may feel they are even more gifted than their pastor and, if given the opportunity, could do a better job. The difference is the pastor is anointed to the office of pastor but the associate is not, at least not at this time, and anxiety is a sure sign you're not ready. At this point, you are called to be an associate and to help your pastor. The associate is called to a time of preparation and service in the ministry where he or she is currently assigned.

There must be certain principles that govern the associate minister as he or she develops into an effective vessel. For those who are frustrated simply because they are seldom used to preach, I assert that pulpit ministry is a very small portion of what ministry really is. The word minister means to serve or, in its most simplistic meaning, to wait on tables. This may not exactly be something we want to shout about, but that's what we are called to do–serve. There are several areas of ministry at the local church level where volunteers are needed. These are areas where the associate minister could volunteer his time and help the ministry move forward. These areas also serve to develop the associate minister in a particular area of ministry.

There may be several reasons why we don't volunteer; however, the real issue is simply "pride." Our idea of ministry is preaching, which means we have misunderstood the true meaning of ministry. If we believe that sitting around waiting for a time to preach is serving, then we have failed to grasp the significance of a powerful example Jesus gave us. In that example, Jesus took a towel and performed a task normally reserved for the servant of the house—He washed the feet of his disciples. That Jesus performed the duties of a servant absolutely stunned the disciples. But it was in His simple demonstration that he illustrated role of the servant leader: to wait on one another, not to be waited on. In so doing, His is our example to follow.

Some associates believe that once called into the ministry, they are above serving. They don't want to gird themselves with the towel of humility and serve others as Jesus did. Some associates want to rule, preach, and have people wait on them, as though they were a deity. I understand the struggles and frustrations of being pregnant without knowing the delivery date; in other words, to have a vision that seems like it will never become a reality. I understand what it feels like to have gifts, talents, dreams, visions, and the desire to have your own ministry. However, we must follow principles and spiritual disciplines if God is going to use us and promote us in His service. These are tests that, if successfully passed, will bring promotions. How do we respond when everyone is being used or promoted, yet we continue to sit? Jesus' call was to those who were already doing something. They were working!

God has taught me several principles and spiritual disciplines throughout the years. These are principles all associate ministers should adopt in order to be blessed where they are now serving and in the ministry God has for them in the future. The principles are purpose, faithfulness, dying, serving with humility, witness, confirmation, sowing and reaping, lines of authority, example, and bearing burdens. I will discuss several within this chapter and others throughout this manual.

Purpose

Why do you attend your current church? After all, didn't you say or feel that God led you there? But now you want to leave. You need to understand that you are at your current church as a direct result of two prayers and the fulfillment of God's purposes. The first prayer is the one your pastor prayed for help to fulfill the vision God placed in his or her heart. The second prayer is the one you prayed for God to prepare you and use you. Both prayers will bring you into a posture of service in a local congregation.

You are also at your current church to fulfill God's purposes. One purpose is to meet the needs of the pastor and local congregation. The other is for the training and preparation of the associate for future ministry. You may not even click with your pastor socially, but you are joined together by the Spirit for the purpose of kingdom building. Both the pastor and the associate ministers need to understand, at the very least, the first two reasons why the associate is currently at the church and under what qualifying factors they may leave. I will discuss reasons for leaving in the section titled "Confirmation."

There are three reasons a person is sent to a church, as far as ministry is concerned. One is to bring temporary help to the local church. If this is the case, you will only be there for a period of time. You probably will never feel comfortable to the point that you really feel at home. God has you there to help meet a need, but you will be moving on at some point in the future.

Secondly, God may have brought you to your church for training. Your time at the church is preparing you for the next level, whatever it may be. There is something that the pastor and ministry have that you need to learn or that needs to be imparted to you—something that you will need wherever God is ultimately leading you. You can also gain valuable experience in the daily operations of the church. Through this experience, the associate can also learn how to minister and handle God's people. These experiences can help teach the associate how to run a church and maintain a ministry.

By learning church operations and how different ministries function, associates will be able to more clearly define their own area of calling and spiritual gifts, and he or she will be more effective for ministry. If you leave prematurely, you will not gain the experience or anointing to effectively minister at the next level. If this happens, you will have to go back and prepare yourself in certain areas of ministry and leadership. If associates leave before time, they will hinder the vision and work at their current church, and also hinder their own destiny.

Thirdly, associates may be a permanent part of the vision. In such a case, the associate is called to a particular ministry and will always be active in some part of the ministry. This means the associate is there for the duration and will never feel comfortable in another church because they will be out of place. Associates will never experience the wealth of God's blessings until they are where they are supposed to be doing what God has called them to do.

In 1Kings 17, God told Elijah to "get thee hence," hide himself, go to a brook where God had commanded a raven to feed him there, arise, and dwell (1Kings 17; 3,4). If Elijah had not obeyed and been in the place where God told him to go, he would have missed God's provision. He was in a place called "there." If he had not been specifically "there," he would not been in place when God came to meet him "there." Get the point? The place of obedience is the place of blessing. Conflict and dissatisfaction are not signs of God having said it's time to leave. Pressure of this sort comes to move us out of position and cause us to leave during times of testing and spiritual development.

We can move out all we want and call it faith. We can even pray and quote all the Scriptures we want. That is not what moves God. Obedience is what moves God—obedience to the place God has called you and submitting to His will for your life. This is the place of blessing. Obedience to the process is the place of blessing.

Most of the time, we move first, and then pray for God's blessing. We need to pray first, receive God's direction, and then move out and do what He has called us to do. You may be on temporary assignment or part of the permanent vision, but the proper time to leave is when God releases you.

Some associates leave their church to start their own ministry because they feel their pastor is not using them. Unfortunately, they usually leave when the pastor and congregation need them most. They leave right at the time the pastor has learned to trust them and is about to delegate more responsibility to them. When associates leave prematurely from where God has them and start a church or ministry, they are usually unskilled, undisciplined, and lack the necessary experience and anointing to do the work required to fulfill the vision. In some cases, this could result in associate totally walking away from the ministry they started. However, if associates continue to work and develop their ministries, they will learn a great deal from their experiences, but will have also lost a valuable amount of training and experience that could have been learned under a seasoned pastor.

Associates must also understand that regardless of how educated, how charismatic, or how well they may preach, if they leave before God's appointed time, they are headed for disaster. Associates may feel that their giftedness and education exceed that of the pastor's. However, the giftedness and abilities possessed by an associate are provided to assist the pastor and ministry, and are part of a gift base for future assignments. The associate's authority and anointing are in direct relation to his or her level of submission to the pastor. These abilities should never be used to bring attention to you, develop a clique, undermine the pastor or steal his or her members. God does not bless mess!

The associate minister should always point the people to the pastor and the vision of the church. Associates are in the same position Aaron and Hur were in Exodus 17, when they lifted up the hands of the pastor (Moses). Aaron and Hur supported leadership in view of all the people. The support of associates should point the people to the pastor by reinforcing what the pastor teaches and preaches. One of the best ways is to let the people see the associate in support of the pastor and the vision of the church. When we know and have accepted our purpose, then we can fully support that purpose. This helps keep unity in the church.

Faithfulness

The Bible has a lot to say about being faithful. However, I want to focus on a passage found in Luke 16:9–13. This Scripture focuses primarily on money. My focus is not on money, but the principle of faithfulness described in the Scripture. Verse 10 states that if a person is faithful in what is little, they will be faithful in much. If God or the pastor cannot trust you to do the little things, they will never promote you to greater responsibilities. My faith test came when as God challenged my motives. You see, I wanted to have my own ministry. I wanted to be "a great man of God." The Lord was leading me to join another man's ministry. I did not want to do that; I wanted to be the one in charge. I wanted to call all the shots. This Scripture tells us that if we are not first faithful in what belongs to another man, God will not give us what belongs to us—our ministries, callings, or gifts.

Several years ago, my family and I were doing ministry with inner city youth. My wife introduced me to a man who was a member of Greenforest Community Baptist Church. As this man and I were talking, he expressed a need he thought the church had in the area of evangelism. Well, I immediately thought this might be God because of my interest and work in the area of evangelism. The church I helped to plant, and where I was currently serving as pastor, did not have the financial backing to remain open. I was paying most of the bills, and had lost my job, so I thought maybe God was giving me a new direction. I decided to visit Greenforest. At first, I did not like the church, nor did I want to be there. However, God's Spirit arrested me and would not give me a release to leave. I could have gone but I would have been in disobedience to God.

One Sunday, Pastor McCalep was preaching a message on spiritual gifts and extended an invitation to come talk to him and let our gifts be known and used. So I did just that. The need for an evangelist leader the brother told me about at Greenforest did not exist. Someone was in that position so, I started working with the evangelism ministry. God began to deal with me about dying to my desires, and becoming faithful in the place where He had placed me. I submitted myself to God and the rest is history.

God has opened many doors and is increasing my borders. All of this is because I was being faithful in another man's vision. The things I dreamed and daydreamed about have become my life. I thought the things God is doing now in my ministry would come later in my life. Being faithful in another man's vision reaped God's response of giving me what belongs to me. Let me add that I am only in the infant stage of His blessings for me. My vision came forth out of the faithfulness in another man's vision.

Dying

In John 12:24–26 Jesus says, *"Verily, verily I say except a corn of wheat fall into the ground and die, it abideth alone: but if it die it brings forth much fruit. He that loveth his life shall lose it; and he that hateth his life in this world shall keep it unto life eternal. If any man serves me, let him follow me."* God's Spirit began to reveal to me that I was just going through the motions, but not dying, planting myself. Even though I was helping at the church, my mind was somewhere else. There were times I would be off somewhere preaching with no desire to be at my church. I wanted to make the circuit and travel the globe. I had a sermon, I knew some Scriptures, and, I could hold my own, as far as preaching, but I had not been prepared spiritually.

As I stated before, I understand how it feels to be sitting in a congregation and have a call of God on your life. Please note that Jesus never called a man who was not doing something. Jesus called the disciples, who were already engaged in some type of employment. If you get busy doing something in the ministry where you are, God will open other doors for you. As I planted myself into the vision at my church, God began to open doors for me. After a year, I was offered a part-time position that seven months later turned into a full-time position. When I died and became faithful from my heart to helping my pastor fulfill God's purpose for him, my vision came out of his vision. My authority and anointing came out of his anointing.

The Joshua Evangelism Ministry was birthed. Books were birthed, consulting positions opened, assisting churches in the area of church growth, evangelism, and associate minister training. I was asked to train African–American churches for the Southern Baptist Convention in North America, Canada, and the Caribbean. I was asked to write an article for the African–American Journal, for the Southern Baptist Convention. I was offered an adjunct professor position to teach urban evangelism at Beulah Heights University in Atlanta, Georgia. Recently, we started a school of evangelism and a school of associate minister training. "Despise not the day of small beginnings" (Zechariah 4:10). God has increased offers to preach, teach seminars, and travel. He has opened doors that have been beyond my dreams.

Can I take my mask off and be truthful? I hesitated to disclose the information above. God has turned me upside down by the processes He has taken me through. There was a time when the things I shared above were a badge of pride for me. I have to be very careful and make sure it is only used to help others or bring glory to God, as in this case. I am afraid to misuse what God has done in and through me, or steal glory that only belongs to Him for the opportunities He has afforded me. Have you ever been chastened by God? I mention my blessings to show you the results of dying to yourself and becoming faithful where you are currently serving.

In John 12:24–26, Jesus taught us to die to our own plans and follow Him. This might mean that you have to plant yourself in another pastor's vision in order for your vision to come forth. If your vision is from God, it will come forth. It will promote His kingdom and bring glory to Him, not to you. My vision grew out of my pastor's vision. If we don't die to our plans, we will never receive God's plan.

Servant

The servant principle has been lost in most churches today. Most associate ministers seek after the high seats, the seats in the pulpit not the seats of service. I was taught, when asked to sit in the pulpit, always take the seat at the end so you do not have to be embarrassed when asked to move. We are no different than the disciples who jockeyed for position (Mark 10:35–38). The associate minister should be a servant leader. Jesus demonstrated this principle to us when He left heaven and took on the form of a man to serve humanity. He was God incarnate coming down to earth to demonstrate to us how servantship should be done.

Sometimes associates struggle with pride, which hinders them from serving. When we stand tall with our chests poked out, it's difficult to exude a posture of service. Jesus is calling us to humble ourselves with the guarantee that we will be exalted (1 Peter 5:6). I suggest that you do things that would help you stay humble and develop within you a servant's heart. Go clean a restroom or pick up paper on the church property. Volunteer to work in the nursery or with children. I guarantee that if you do, it will help you stay humble. I have friends who are pastors and they tell me they have a hard time getting the associate ministers in their churches to volunteer to do anything. Most times, when they are asked to do something, they want to be financially compensated for services rendered. Some of these churches have ministers who sit in the pulpit every Sunday waiting for a chance to preach. Some of them are not involved in any ministry of the church. I think, at the very least, every associate minister should teach a Sunday School class and attend Bible study.

God has called us to be servants. As associate ministers, we are called to serve the pastor and God's people. Serving is not preaching alone; serving is doing what needs to be done to support God's vision in the ministry where we serve. In doing this, associates will position themselves for great things in the service of the Lord and for promotion.

Associate's Introspection

As you reflect on the content of this lesson, what is God saying to you?

1. What do you perceive your role is as an associate minister?

_____

_____

_____

_____

_____

2. Are you dead to your own purpose?

_____

_____

_____

_____

_____

3. Are you waiting on a time to preach?

_____

_____

_____

_____

_____

4. What are some of the constraints on the relationship between you and your pastor?

_____

_____

_____

_____

_____

5. In what other areas can you serve outside the pulpit?

_____

_____

_____

_____

_____

_____

6. What concerns do you have regarding your lack of being used in ministry by your pastor?

_____

_____

_____

_____

_____

_____

7. List some of the suggestions given to the associate to help open doors of ministry. Which ones can you personally use?

_____

_____

_____

_____

_____

_____

8. List ways you can help in the ministry in which you currently serve?

_____

_____

_____

_____

_____

_____

The Call of the Associate Minister

I remember years ago how I desired to be called to preach. I thought preaching was the only calling in the church. At least it was the only call to which I aspired. My desire was to preach because of the prestige that went with the position. God did call me a few years later, but along with the call He showed me the responsibility and accountability that went with the call. Once He did this, it changed my outlook of ministry. He also showed me that ministry is more than preaching, it's serving.

The call to preach is not a call to a lavish lifestyle where members cater to the every need of the preacher, nor is it a calling to preach only. It is a calling to serve God as we serve others, something lacking among some associate ministers. I am not trying to be hard on associate ministers. There has been a lack of education in these areas, so most associates do not know what to do as far as service. Most associates only act out what they see. If we're honest, what has been demonstrated by a number of pastors is a lifestyle rather than a serving style.

As associates, we are to minister to others. As I previously stated, to minister means to wait on tables or serve. Pulpit ministry is only a small portion of ministry. Some associates desire a position only–the position of pastor. Some associates act like their only calling is to sit in the pulpit and wait on the next opportunity to preach. God always calls people who are doing something. He does not call people who are lazy or looking for a position only. Jesus called disciples who were already doing something. Paul was already doing something when he was called.

In most cases, God takes something a person is already doing, lifts up the natural gift or vocation of the person, and uses it for ministry. Are you sitting around just waiting for an opportunity to preach? Then God is calling you. The call, however, is not to preach, but to repent. If you are an associate waiting for a call to preach, be assured God is calling, but there are other calls before He calls you to preach or pastor.

The first call, of associate ministers after salvation, is to their spiritual development. Powerful ,anointed ministry flows out of intimacy with God. Time spent in prayer and God's Word should not only be during times of preparing to preach or teach, but daily.

As we approach God we should use the following steps:

1. Give God first fruits (Mark 1:35).
2. Enter God's presence through the name of Jesus (John 14:13; Hebrews 9:12).
3. Confess known or unknown sin in our lives (1 John 1:9).
5. Enter His gate with thanksgiving because of who He is. Enter into His court with praise for what He has done.

Cultivating Intimacy with God:

Associates aspire to be fruitful in God's service. This involves cultivating intimacy with Almighty God through spiritual development. It is the very character of forming and maintaining a deeply personal relationship with Him. In so doing associates abide in God and invite His abiding in us (John 15:4,5). This involves associates doing the following:

A. Come before His Presence
    *   Through Jesus (John 14:13, Hebrews 9:12)
    *   With singing (Psalms 95:1; 100:2)
    *   With thanksgiving (Psalms 95:2)
    *   With thanksgiving and praise (Psalms 100:4)
    *   In worship (Psalms 95:6)
    *   Giving the glory due Him (Psalms 96:8)
    *   Blessing His name (Psalms 100:4)
    *   With fear (Psalms 96:9)
    *   Bowing down in humility (Psalms 95:6)
    *   Kneeling before Him (Psalms 95:6)

B. Know
    *   He is God (Psalms 100:3).
    *   He has made us, not we ourselves (Psalms 100:3).
    *   We are His people, and the sheep of His pasture (Psalms 100:3).
    *   He is a great God, and a great King above all gods (Psalms 95:3).
    *   In His hand are the deep places of the earth: the strength of the hills is His also (Psalms 95:4).
    *   He is great, and greatly to be praised (Psalms 96:4).
    *   He is to be feared above all gods (Psalms 96:4).
    *   All other gods of the nations are idols (Psalms 96:5).
    *   Honor and majesty are before Him: strength and beauty are in his sanctuary (Psalms 96:6).

C. Repent
- Warning against a hard heart (Psalms 95:8–11). Israel saw His works but did not know His ways and refused to glorify Him for his deeds, (Psalms 95:10–11).
- Admit sin against God–Confession (Psalms 51; Proverbs 28:13; James 5:16 and 1 John 1:9).

D. Commune
- Commune with God through praise, prayer, worship, and meditation (Psalms 100:4, Matthew 6:9, Luke 4:8, Joshua 1:8).
- Surrender that which He has given to us (Romans 12:1).
- Give yourself back to Him willingly for service (John 4:34).
- Esteem His Word. Job said, he esteemed God's word more than his necessary food (Job 23:12).
- Dedicate ourselves to accomplishing what He has called us to do (Luke 23:46).

I like to use the pattern of the tabernacle as a guide to entering God's presence and as an example of church. First, we wash the sin of Adam that brought death upon all men. Our sin is satisfied and atoned through Jesus Christ. In the tabernacle, the sacrifice was at the brazen alter and was a type of Christ that would come. The next piece of furniture was the laver. This is where the priests washed their hands and feet. The priest would see their reflection in mirrors from which the Laver was made. We are a kingdom of priests (Revelations 1:6). We need to wash ourselves from daily sin before entering God's presence. The priest would wash their hands and feet. Likewise, we need to wash away what our hands have done, and where our feet have been. We cannot enter if sin is in our lives. We must also confess sin daily. The brazen alter is for atonement and the laver is for sanctification, which is the process of spiritual development. After we are cleansed from sin we can enter into His presence. From there, we can move behind the veil and into intimacy with God. God desires to have intimacy with us. He is not holding sin over our heads. In fact, the only thing He is holding over our head is the word "come."

The second call associate minister receives from God is a call to family. How can associates preach to others if their family is not being ministered to? What kind of example can you be to others if your family is lacking physically, spiritually, and financially? Associates must first be partakers of God's Word. In other words, we must live what we preach before others, and that begins with our families first.

We have to be careful how we live because our lives may be the only Bible others read. We cannot be a stumbling block to others who might be leaning towards receiving Christ, but choose not to because of our hypocrisy. We must first live out the biblical principles we communicate to others, among our families members. This means that associates must protect, provide for and guide their family members. This responsibility was first given to Adam, the spiritual head of God's first family.

Most ministers encounter family problems because they put church and ministry before family. However, family is your first responsibility and ministry. The order should be God first, that is your personal relationship with Him, not the church. Your spouse and children are next. After that is the church, and last is, your vocation. If a pastor is bi-vocational, however, work may need to come before church. In such cases, if the pastor is paying all the bills and does not work, the church will not survive. So, work might come before church in this case.

Let me step to the side to speak to male associates because the male is the priest of the home. The male associate should lead his family in devotion and spiritual matters. He should be the priest of his home, leading his family in the things of God. He should be a provider, and his family should not need to worry about their natural needs being met. It does not go over well if we can meet everyone else's needs, but cannot meet the needs of our own family.

I have a friend who is a pastor. He told me his wife suggested that she become a church member and step down from the position of the pastor's wife because then she would be more likely to have her needs responded to by her pastor. This was her way of telling him that he was placing the members needs before his own family. Some associates have put church before spouse and family. This is one of the reasons why so many preachers have lost their children. They placed the church before their children. As a result, the children resent the church and do not want anything to do with church as adults.

Sometimes we get things a bit out of order when it comes to church, our spouse, and family. We say, "I have to go to church," or something church related. We put family second to members and church functions. As a result, we lose our children, spouse, and family. There are some ministers who have lost their jobs because they put church before work. Listen! If you have a family and walk off your job because you are scheduled to work at the same time your church service occurs, is this faith or foolishness? I suggest your responsibility is to take care of your family first. Do this first, and God will bless you. But, if you quit your job you have opened the door for Satan to bring hardships upon your family.

I believe that a minister should be at church on Sunday. However, if you have a job where you have to work Sundays, do not quit and call it "stepping out on faith." Continue to work, look and believe God for another job before leaving the one you are on. You may put your family in the position of needing assistance from the church, which may be embarrassing to you.

As an associate, do not be so busy with church duties that you neglect your responsibilities as a husband or wife. You can never get back those special moments when you miss your children's functions. God is about family; it's your first ministry. If the minister's home is in shambles, then how can he/she effectively minister or witness to others?

Associates must also provide biblical guidance to the family unit in practical and spiritual matters. Sometimes the only time we find ourselves in God's Word is when we are asked to preach. Yet, God has a daily Word for you in your personal life and family. Do you only pray when it is your time to preach? God expects you to also pray for your family and engage in spiritual warfare on their behalf when Satan attacks. They must see you walk in the Word and Godly character, which will demonstrate a spiritual example to your wife and children. This is your first ministry before you lead others or minister from the pulpit. Ministry and character start at home.

What is character? In simple terms it is who you really are. It is how you act and what you do when others are not around. Character is how associates act in the absence of family, church members, and the pastor. Do you live one way at church and another way at home? Would your wife and children say you live like the devil at home? Do your family members witness a different person at home than the one they see in the pulpit? Have you destroyed your witness to your own family?

The qualifications for the office of the pastor found in 1 Timothy Chapter 3 are what associates should be striving for also. Associates are to be:

- above reproach.
- the husband of one wife.
- temperate.
- prudent.
- hospitable.
- able to teach.
- not addicted to wine.
- not quarrelsome.
- gentle, uncontentious.
- lovers of God, not love money.
- managers of their household.
- experienced, not a novice.
- of good reputation.

Titus Chapter 1 continues the list of qualifications. Associates are to be:
- submissive, not self-willed.
- patient, not quick-tempered.
- lovers of what is good.
- just.
- devout.
- self-controlled.

These are the spiritual disciplines we are to practice at home before we preach to others. You and I will always be working on them but we must continue to do so, at home first.

The third calling associate ministers receive is a call to prepare for ministry. This call is first and foremost a call of intimacy with God through fasting, praying, and the study of His Word. Then, training comes as one is educated while working in another person's ministry, attending Bible school or seminary, experiencing life, and enduring the spiritual development process.

I shared earlier about the call and education process the associates gain by planting themselves in another's ministry. One does not have to do all this before one preaches or is used by the pastor. It is a continuous process of discipline and learning. I believe it is important for the associate ministers to prepare in both an academic setting and by personal spiritual development. There must be a balance between academics and one's experiences. I believe balance is the key. Someone who has the letter (education) without the Spirit is not balanced. Likewise, someone who emphasizes Spirit without the letter is also not balanced.

Jesus was God in the flesh (you can't get more Spirit than that), yet He learned from His parents, teachers of the law, and nature. I believe the Spirit and the natural make a associates balanced and allows them to be more effective for God's use.

Associates must always be students of learning. We are in the ministry to teach, preach, and counsel people, so we must continue to prepare ourselves and be students of the Word of God and other venues of education.

On the next page is a ministerial track that may help pastors train their associates. The track can be modified to best contextualize or reflect the personal needs of your congregation. The purpose of the track is to educate associates cognitively and experientially. Knowledge learned will greatly benefit the pastor, church, and associate. Secondly, it will prepare associates for next level ministry.

Ministerial Training Track

Introduction
(Eight Weeks)
Roles, Expectation and Commitment Module 1
Book, *Keys to Becoming an Effective Associate Minister and Pastor"*

Section Two
(Two weeks)
Salvation Counseling
Commitment Counseling Manual

Section Three
(Two weeks)
Evangelism Training
All ministers must attend.

Section Four
(One week)
Visitation Do's and Don'ts
All candidates must complete two visits

Section Five
(One week)
Funerals Visitations Sermons and Grave Site Services

Section Six
(Three weeks)
Sermon Preparation
Book, *"Power In The Pulpit"*
All candidates must prepare two sermons.

Section Seven
(Five weeks)
Denominational Beliefs and Doctrines

Section Eight
Written Papers (Pastor's Assignments)
Major Doctrines of the Church

Section Nine
Spiritual Gifts/ Spiritual Growth Assessment
Candidates Teach or Read material on this subject

Section Ten
Ministry Practicum
Each associate will spend at least one hour working weekly in a ministry of the church.

Section Eleven
Supervised Visits and Funerals

Section Twelve
Preparation for License or Ordination

NOTE: After completion of the ministerial track and before ordination, all ministerial candidates will be assigned a duty or Sunday School class.

Associates desire greatly to be used in ministry. We lose them when they are not utilized, or don't feel a part of the church's ministry. When one actively engages in doing or training, one then feels a sense of belonging. This is key because it assures the pastor they will be faithful and that they have taken ownership or bought into his or her vision.

Questions

1. What does accountability and responsibility mean to you?

_____

_____

_____

_____

_____

_____

_____

2. Name and discuss the calls of the associate minister.

_____

_____

_____

_____

_____

_____

_____

3. List the order of priorities in the associate's life.

_____

_____

_____

_____

_____

_____

_____

4. What should associates provide for their families?

_____

_____

_____

_____

_____

_____

_____

5. What things can I do to improve my character?

_____

_____

_____

_____

_____

_____

_____

6. Discuss the spiritual disciplines found in 1 Timothy 3 and Titus 1.

_____

_____

_____

_____

_____

_____

_____

All Ministers should know how to present the gospel to the lost. When we share the gospel, the message should be inviting, giving hope and causing a response, even if it is negative. Remember, you are only called to plant a seed or sprinkle water on a seed that has already been planted. God gives the increase. Do not be discouraged if you do not see immediate results. God rewards obedience, and you have done that by planting a seed. The unbeliever's response is not toward you, but God.

When you share the gospel message, as I stated above, you're telling a love story. Remember, you are communicating how Jesus changed your life and gave you a hope beyond the grave. You are not trying to sell your church. Most unbelievers are turned off by our churches. The power of Christ can deliver them, so share Jesus and His power.

The message should have the following five points:

1. God's Purpose

    a. God wants us to have a better life now (John 10:10).

    b. God also wants us to have eternal life, but there is a problem called sin (John 3:16).

2. Our Sin Nature

    a. Sin keeps us from what God has for us (Genesis 3).

    b. Adam's sin was passed on to all men (Romans 5:12).

    c. All have sinned (Romans 3:23).

    d. Sin demands judgment , so we must repent (Romans 6:23)!

3. Repentance and Faith Alone

    a. God commands all men to repent (Acts 17:30).

    b. Repent and be converted (Acts 3:19).

    c. We are saved by grace through faith, not by works (Ephesians. 2:8–9).

4. God's Plan

    a. God came in the flesh in the person of Jesus Christ (John 1:14).

    b. Christ suffered for our sins (1 Peter 3:18).

    c. God laid our sin on Jesus (Isaiah 53:6).

    e. You cannot save them, but you can lead them in a prayer, and if they mean the prayer from their heart, they will be saved.

5.   Surrender and Acceptance of Christ

  a. God gives us the power to become His sons or daughters (John 1:12).

  b. You must believe in your heart and confess with your mouth that Jesus is Lord of your life (Romans 10:9–10).

  c. Ask if they understand everything you say. If not, clarify!

  d. Ask them if they are ready to pray.

  e. You cannot save them, but you can lead them in a prayer, and if they mean the prayer from their hearts, they will be saved.

  f. The prayer should consist of three elements:

   (1) Acknowledging of sin, not trying to list all sin, just being truly sorry for all sins committed.

   (2) Asking God to forgive you of all your sin.

   (3) Accepting of Christ

Are you
a
Servant Leader?

The Role of the Pastor

We do not have to look any further than 1 Peter 5:1–3 to find the foundational principles of pastoral leadership: feed the flock; take charge, not using force; do not let money be the motive for which you serve; and serve as an example to all people. The Bible uses the term shepherd many times. The term describes a spiritual leader who protects and guides a flock into green pastures. The feeding and protection of the sheep are the essential duties of the shepherd's calling. The shepherd is not to feed the sheep nourishment that is unhealthy, but, rather, that which nourishes their souls. It is the responsibility of the shepherd to preach and teach God's Word to the sheep. The shepherd should protect the flock from predators that will lead them astray or feed them the wrong diet. Above all, the list is extensive concerning the things a pastor should do and be. In his book, *Pastoral Ministry,* John MacArthur describes a philosophy of ministry of being and doing, detailed by the Apostle Paul in both epistles to Timothy, his spiritual son. According to the Book of 1 Timothy, the pastor's role is to:

- Correct those teaching false doctrine and call them to a pure heart, a good conscience, and a sincere faith (1:3–5).
- Fight for divine truth and for God's purpose, keeping his own faith and a good conscience (1:1–19).
- Pray for the lost and lead other men to do the same (2:1–8).
- Call women in the church to fulfill their God-given role of submission and to raise up godly children, setting an example of faith, love, and sanctity with self-restraint (2:9–15).
- Carefully select spiritual leaders for the church on the basis of their giftedness, godliness, and virtue (3:1–13).
- Recognize any sources of error and those who teach them, and point these things out to the rest of the church (4:1–6).
- Constantly be nourished on the words of the Scripture and its sound teaching, avoiding all myths and false doctrines (4:6).
- Discipline himself for the purpose of godliness (4:1–11).
- Boldly command and teach the truth of God's Word (4:12).

- Be a model of spiritual virtue that all can follow (4:12).
- Faithfully read, explain, and apply the Scriptures publicly (4:13–14).
- Progress toward Christ-likeness in his own life (4:15–16).
- Be gracious and gentle in confronting the sin of his people (5:1–2).
- Give special consideration and care to those who are widows (5:3–16).
- Honor faithful church leaders who work hard (5:17–21).
- Choose church leaders with great care, seeing to it that they are both mature and proven (5:22).
- Take care of his physical condition so he is strong and able to serve (5:23).
- Teach and preach principles of godliness, helping his people discern between true godliness and mere hypocrisy (5:24–6:6).
- Flee the love of money (6:7–11).
- Pursue righteousness, godliness, faith, love, perseverance, and gentleness (6:11).
- Fight for the faith against all enemies and attacks (6:12).
- Instruct others to be rich in good works and to be generous (6:17–19).
- Guard the Word of God as a sacred treasure (6:12).

In his second epistle, Paul reminded Timothy to:

- Keep the gift of God in him fresh and useful (1:6).
- Not be timid but powerful (1:7).
- Never be ashamed of Christ or anyone who serves Him (1:8–11).
- Hold tight to the truth and guard it (1:1–14).
- Be strong in character (2:1).
- Be a teacher of truth so that he may reproduce himself in faithful men (2:2).
- Suffer difficulty and persecution willingly while making the maximum effort for Christ (2:3–7).
- Keep his eyes on Christ at all times (2:8–13).
- Lead with authority (2:14).
- Interpret and apply Scripture accurately (2:15).
- Avoid useless conversations that lead only to ungodliness (2:16).
- Be an instrument of honor, set apart from sin and useful to the Lord (2:20–21).
- Flee youthful lust and pursue righteousness, faith, and love (2:22).
- Refuse to be drawn into philosophical and theological wrangling (2:23).

- Don't argue, but be kind, teachable, gentle, and patient, even when wronged (2:24–26).
- Face dangerous times with a deep knowledge of the Word of God (3:1–15).

In his book, *The Effective Pastor*, Robert Anderson lists certain biblical character qualifications which apply to the pastor. The first quality is that one should be above reproach (1 Timothy 3:2; Titus 1:6–7). This means that there should not be any skeletons or hidden agendas Anderson goes on to state that the pastor should be the husband of one wife (1 Timothy 3:2; Titus 1:6).

Temperance is another quality needed to be a workman in God's kingdom (1 Timothy 3:2). Temperance is using self-control in all areas of life. Moderation is the key. Prudence is the next quality that a workman should possess. To be prudent means to not engage in behavior that is knowingly offensive to others; to not be loud, rude or boisterous in places and situations where such behavior is not acceptable. Another quality is to be respectable or of good behavior (1 Timothy 3:2). The meaning here is to have orderliness of personality, modesty, and decorum. Teachers who often function in the office of an evangelist, need to not only be able to communicate the gospel, but teach others (1 Timothy 3:2; 2 Timothy 2:24). To not be addicted to wine (1 Timothy 3:3; Titus 1:7), no doubt is referring to those who are habitual users of wine or, in our day, drugs as well.

Another quality is that we are not to be pugnacious (1 Timothy 3:3; Titus 1:7), which speaks of one who likes to fight. As a Christian, especially one in leadership, one's attitude should always be like Christ's. Gentleness is another quality that the Scriptures refer to as an attribute of Christian character (1 Timothy 3:3; 2 Timothy 2:24). Anderson goes on to mention contentiousness. Unlike pugnacious a contentious person is someone who lives to argue (1 Timothy 3:3; 2 Timothy 2:24). One should be free from the love of money (1 Timothy 3:3; Titus 1:7). A leader must also be able to manage his household well (1 Timothy 3:4). The position of pastor is reserved for someone seasoned in the faith—not a new convert (1 Timothy). The pastor should have a good reputation with those who are outside of the church (1 Timothy 3:7). Anderson goes on to say that pastors should not be resentful when wronged (2 Timothy 2:24).

A leader's children are required to be in check, not self-willed or quick-tempered (Titus 1:6). Verse 8 of Titus Chapter 1 lists four more qualities: a lover of that which is good, just, devout, and one who exercises self-control. Above all this, the pastor is expected to fulfill ministerial tasks.

The pastor's life is filled with long hours, and they sometimes receive very little appreciation. The pastor is expected to be all things to all people. The pastor is expected to:

- Teach
- Preach
- Lead service
- Open the church doors
- Close the church doors
- Counsel
- Perform weddings
- Perform funerals
- Visit the sick
- Visit those in nursing homes
- Visit those in the hospital
- Make home visits
- Attend board meetings
- Settle disputes
- Bail members out of financial problems
- Prepare sermons
- Conduct church business
- Have a community presence
- Conduct all types of church services
- Visit prisons
- Read and meditate
- Pray
- Perform the Lord's Supper and Baptisms
- Perform children's services and dedications
- Plan and manage
- Respond to correspondence
- Lead building programs

Above all these things, the pastor has to maintain a devotional life and the care of his family. The role of the pastor is tough. The call is challenging and the life is one of tremendous sacrifice. No one truly understands the long hours, late night phone calls and visits, except their family members.

"Go into all the world."Some of us may have the witness of the Spirit. In other words, we have this deep feeling on the inside that God has called us into ministry or a specific area of calling.

However, the one that most of us miss is the witness of our circumstances. This occurs when our circumstances do not line up. In other words, the timing is not right, and we try to birth something prematurely. We either leave with no experience, or we leave because we feel we have all the experience we need. However, to leave in either case would be unwise. Joshua understood these principles.

In Deuteronomy 31:1–15, Moses told the children of Israel that he was old and could not continue to lead them. He assured them that God was going to give them the land. However, it would not be under his leadership, but it would be under the leadership of Joshua. Moses was God's spokesman. He was the Word of God to the people. At this point, Joshua was given God's Word through Moses. He was called to lead the people, but not at that moment. This was God's word to him.

In Deuteronomy 31:14, God told Moses to have Joshua go to the tabernacle of the congregation. The Lord appeared in the tabernacle in a pillar of a cloud that stood over the door. The visible cloud was the witness or confirmation of God's Spirit. At this point, Joshua had the witness of the Word of God and the Spirit of God. This is when most associates leave to start their own ministries. Joshua never left even though he had a witness of the Word and the Spirit of God. We do not see Joshua going over to the other side of the desert and starting another church. He could have, for he was trained and experienced. He had leadership abilities and there was probably a group of people who would have followed him. Instead, Joshua remained faithful to Pastor Moses and to the congregation—the children of Israel.

It was not until Joshua 1 that Joshua's circumstances lined up with his situation. God spoke to him and told him that Moses was dead, and it was his time to lead. His circumstances now lined up. He now had the witness of God's Word, the witness of God's Spirit, and his circumstances agreed with his appointment to leadership. Joshua may have been tempted, but he never took a group to the other side of the Sinai desert and started another church.

There are six other reasons that indicate a proper time for associates to leave the current church where they are serving. The first two are found in Acts 13:1–2. Where the Spirit of God gave confirmation and confirmation by spiritual authority. "Now there were in the church that was at Antioch certain prophets and teachers. As they ministered to the Lord and fasted, the Holy Ghost said, "Separate me Barnabas and Saul for the work whereunto I have called them.""

Notice that the Spirit of God will confirm His purpose to those in authority. When it is time for you to leave where you are serving, the pastor should also know that it is time for you to move on and should have no problem releasing you. Associates should never leave on the word of someone else. A word of confirmation is the only word that should be received from someone other than the associate's covering.

The third reason for associates to leave a church is that their gifts open doors that bring them before great men (Proverbs 18:16). As a result you do not have to make calls, pass out cards trying to get an engagement or politic. God knows right where you are, and when the fullness of time comes, He will open doors for you.

When it was time for Israel to have a king, God chose Saul. Samuel caused all the tribes of Israel to come before the Lord by thousands to see God's choice. Out of all the thousands of people Saul was chosen, but he was nowhere to be found. He hid himself. God knew where he was, and chose him out of all those thousands. When it is your time, God will find you. Psalm 139 says that we can go to heaven or hell but we cannot flee from the presence of God. There is no hiding place when God calls you. Even if we, like Saul, are hiding in the stuff.

The fourth reason is due to natural circumstance, such as job relocation, marriage, the care of a family member, or other things of this nature. Sometimes our circumstances will dictate a change. I have a friend who decided to move his family to another city for ministry without God leading him. In one year he was back in Atlanta. He said it was the worst year of his life. Every door was closed to him and he had to come back to the original place where God was developing him.

The fifth reason for associates to leave a church would be if another ministry sought you. Notice I said they sought you and you did not seek them. Even in this circumstance you still need to seek God to confirm it is His will for your life. Position and money do not authenticate that it is God's will for you. If you went looking, you still need to seek God. I have had other ministries offer me positions. Yes, I have been offered more money and other amenities. However, I try to govern my life by Colossians 3:15, which says to let the "peace of God rule in your heart." It means to let the peace of God be an umpire in your heart. In other words, if you do not have peace about your decision, the umpire is calling you 'out.' If you do not have peace on the inside, God is calling you out, and you have just walked out of His will for your life. Peace means you are in God's will.

The final reason is by the pastor's agreement. Some will not agree, but out of respect and because the pastor is the watchman for your soul, the pastor should know. When you feel like the Holy Spirit is leading you to leave, and the pastor also bears witness, the pastor should have no problem releasing you. Leaving without the approval of spiritual authority would be wrong.

If you have a pastor who is not open to your leaving and refuses to acknowledge your vision, seek the peace of God; just do not get mad and frustrated and leave in the wrong way. Pray, then sit down and talk with your pastor. Share your vision and desire to leave, but please do not leave mad or in the wrong spirit. If you have gone to the pastor with the right spirit and he or she acts possessive and just wants to hold onto you, then I would strongly recommend leaving, as long as the peace of God confirms and releases you. If you leave in the wrong manner you will only have to come back and get it right, or you will start a ministry that will never progress. If you seek to do what is right, in due season, God will give you a release to go or stay.

You can be assured that the itch to leave will come. However, if you apply these principles, you will be blessed and will be a blessing to the pastor and the congregation where you currently serve. The way you serve and the way you leave will produce associates in your ministry of the same character (Galatians 6). You reap what is sown.

Questions

1. What is the best position for a church to be in, in the event of the untimely death of a pastor?

_____

_____

_____

_____

_____

2. Explain the term "Don't scratch the itch." Do you have an itch to leave where you are currently serving?

_____

_____

_____

_____

_____

3. Name three principles most associates miss when it is time to leave a ministry.

_____

_____

_____

_____

_____

4. Name six reasons that indicate it is appropriate time to leave a church, and explain them.

_____

_____

_____

_____

_____

5. Name one Scripture associates can use to secure God's peace within, when making decisions.

_____

_____

_____

_____

_____

_____

_____

Ceremonies and Functions of the Church

Leaders are called to serve God's people. The leader's role is to provide leadership in spiritual matters and to carry out ceremonies and duties of the church. In this lesson we will discuss the duties and simulate functional performance.

While churches vary in duties and functions, a basic knowledge and grasp of the functions are the objective of this lesson. In addition, we understand some ceremonies, duties, and functions are reserved for the pastor, ordained clergy or those appointed by the pastor appoints. We intend to provide a basic knowledge for associates and a guide for pastors who might use this manual for training associates. Those who continue next semester will receive more instruction in these areas as well as the major doctrines of the church and sermon development. All ministers should own a copy of *Christian Minister Manual*, which gives a great amount of additional information in these and other areas.

Baptisms

Baptism is the first of two ordinances of the church, the other being communion. These ordinances are sacred rites (sacraments) recognized as of particular importance and significance. Baptism identifies us with Christ's death. Candidates should be properly instructed in the prerequisites of baptism and its Scriptural meaning before administering the ordinance. The person administering baptism should stand on the left side and somewhat to the rear of the candidate. With his right hand raised, the minister pronounces the charge, slowly lowering the candidate into the water. Candidates should be lowered until their entire bodies are submerged. We suggest the candidate's nose and mouth be covered with a cloth.

Communion

Communion is the second ordinance of the church. Jesus himself gave us the Lord's Supper using the simple elements representing His body and blood, we have a memorial from what He did as he served elements to His disciples. As we partake in the elements, we look back upon His sacrifice, receive forgiveness for our sins, receive healing, and substantiate our hope of His return. Usually the communion table is placed in full view of the congregation.

The elements Jesus used were bread and wine. Most churches substitute grape juice and some kind of bread, wafer, or cracker. Instructions relative to receiving the elements should be given based on 1 Corinthians 11:27–32. Elements are handled by ordained deacons or ministers. Prayer is given over the elements before they are distributed to the congregation. From the pulpit or communion table, the pastor will conduct the ceremony according to 1 Corinthians 11:23–26. He will take the bread and juice and quote verse 23–24. Taking the juice, the process will be repeated quoting from verse 25. After the congregants receive the elements, the pastor will pray, the congregation will sing a hymn, and then dismissal.

Some churches observe foot washing as part of the communion process. The service can be observed during communion or during a different service. The Scripture reference for foot washing is found in John 13:1–17.

Dedications and Ordination

Dedications are one of the duties carried out by the pastor or associate. The following are types of dedications.
- Buildings (1 Kings 8)
- Ground-breaking
- Babies (Mark)
- Furniture for Christian work
- Christian workers for service

Ordination is a service where the local church declares that one has earned the right to serve as a minister of the gospel or Christian work. Ordination services are held for deacons, ministers, and elders, and should never be taken lightly. Dedication sets one apart for God's use and service. Candidates for dedication are usually observed by leadership and the local congregation before being considered for ordination. The candidate's faith, character, and practice are observed. Before ordination, the candidate usually appears before a catechism committee to ascertain the candidate's knowledge of scripture and the duties of the office he or she will enter.

Funerals

Funerals are a difficult task but part of the ministry and responsibility of ministers and associates. I want to suggest some things that will help during times of great pain. These things are for general knowledge and should be done if the pastor is not present.

It is important to respond as soon as possible upon hearing of the passing of a member.

Upon hearing of a death immediately inform the pastor. This may not be possible at all times. However, call the pastor as soon as possible.

If a phone call is made to the family, communicate your condolences. For example you might say, "I am so sorry to hear of your loss." Secondly, ask if there are any needs they have at that time. Tell them you will be coming by later and pray for them. I do not believe you should tell them you know how they feel. You may have lost a father, mother, brother, sister, uncle, aunt, brother-in-law, sister-in-law, child, or whomever, but your feeling and depth of loss may not be equivalent to theirs. Never tell them they will get over the death of a loved one. They will live on after the loss of their loved one but they may carry the scars throughout life. A person has the right to grieve! It is part of life. It is a process and the length of the process depends on the person grieving. Certainly, to grieve to the point that you cannot function in life is not healthy. A healthy grieving process should always bring a person back to normalcy of life.

Thirdly, ask if they have selected a funeral home. If so, write down the information so it can be communicated to the pastor and church office. If the death occurs at the hospital and you are present, give the family time to say their good-byes. Allow them privacy without your presence, unless they ask you to remain. Pray with the family. Don't try to make plans or arrangements at this time. The family needs this time and possibly the next few days to process and reflect on the events that have occurred. You can let them know that you will contact them later or will accompany them when they go to make the arrangements. Offer to call relatives and friends, if they need assistance. Most of all, just be there. Your presence means more than anything you could do at this point. It is not what you say during this time, but just being there. It is not a time of response. Your listening will help the most.

There are several events that occur during and after death that the associate should know.

- **Arrangements for the deceased:** When family members visit the funeral home to make final arrangements, it is recommended that a minister goes along for support to help in this phase. During this time family members may feel some form of guilt if they do not, "put their family member away right." I said it that way for a reason. It's what we hear family members say. This means, "I need to spend a lot of money," and sometimes the funeral home will play on this. Help members or at least offer to help them make wise decisions..

- **Home visitation:** Friends and family will usually assemble at one home and receive guests. Don't ask, "how are you doing?" Let them know you came by to support them and serve them. How can I help? It is always appropriate to take some kind of food item, paper towels, napkins, and something to drink. Breakfast items and toilet paper are needed items that people often don't think about.

- **Wake:** A wake is a service where those who knew the deceased will visit the church or funeral home to pay their final respects. This service is usually held the day or night before the funeral.
- **Funeral Service:** The funeral service begins with a procession. However, the family may elect to already be seated. The family is free to plan the service. I suggest the minister offer help. The minister knows what is acceptable and what is not acceptable. You want the service to be orderly and Christian in nature. The pastor, minister, and sometimes dignitaries, lead the precession. The pastor or associate will stand in the pulpit until all family members have viewed the body. After everyone is seated, he or she will give the order of service. The order of service consists of prayer, reading Scripture, an Old Testament passage and a New Testament passage. Psalms 91 or Psalms 23 are two favorites from the Old Testament and John 14:1–6, 1 Thessalonians 4:1–18 from the New Testament. The scripture reading will be followed by prayer, song, remarks, song, eulogy, and acknowledgments, which may include a resolution and dismissal.
- **Internment:** Interment is performed at the burial site when the body is committed to the ground. A prayer, song, reading of Scripture, usually Revelations 21:1–7, and committal of the body are usually done. Sometimes, before or after the committal service, military personal will perform military honors which will include the folding of the United States flag, and Taps. After the committal, the service should be turned back into the hands of the funeral director.
- **Repast:** A repast is a time of expressing condolences and fellowship with the family. This occurs at the church or the home of the deceased or family member after the internment. It can be held anywhere.
- **Grave-side Service:** The family may elect to have the service at the grave and not at church. This may occur in the case of a child or someone who was not a Christian. Keep in mind there are different services and sermons for children, and nonbelievers. Funerals occur at day, at night, and at sea. As I stated above, a minister's manual will help in these areas.

Memorial Service

Memorial services occur due to different circumstances. This is often the case if the deceased is well known, but the funeral is held in a location of considerable distance away from the community in which he/she lived. Secondly, some may have a memorial service to pay tribute to someone. Thirdly, if the body will be cremated, the family may prefer a memorial service. Fourthly, the family may desire a private service. Finally a memorial service is held when the body is not present.

Most pastors love to have assistance during funeral services. Associates can help and should be prepared to read a Scripture, pray, lead a song, or anything asked including assisting with the internment. Usually, there is sufficient help at the funeral, but not at the grave site.

The best way to learn is by doing. I believe this should be part of the associate's training. It's hard to carry out the duties of your office if no one will teach you. The knowledge and experience you gain will help the existing church and the minister as you assume greater leadership responsibilities.

I thank God for the training I received at Greenforest Community Baptist Church. I attended a funeral once, where the minister called to say that he was held up in traffic. He said he was going to be at least another twenty minutes. I was the liturgist, the person who leads the service, or master of ceremonies. The family, who was standing outside ready to march in, asked if I could conduct the service. With God's help, I did. I have conducted several family members' funerals. This would never have been possible without on-the-job training at my church.

Pastoral Care

When I use the term "pastoral care," I am referring to the care of the congregation. This includes, calling the sick; visiting the sick at home, hospitals, nursing homes, or in hospice care; and visiting those who are incarcerated. We are to care for widows and orphans. We are to also carry communion to members who may not be able to attend worship service. I believe churches should also extend visitation to non-active members.

When visiting a medical facility, always sanitize your hands upon entering and exiting the building. Do not visit if you are sick. When visiting the sick or elderly, limit your time to around twenty minutes.

Worship Service

Each church has its own worship style. Associates should not enter the pulpit to serve without having a general knowledge of the worship style and order of service. This does not apply to visiting other churches. I suggest associates learn the order of service, prepare a Scripture if called upon to read, and be spiritually prepared to pray, which means you should have taken care of personal sins before entering the pulpit.

Also have money in case you are asked to lift the offering. Participate in the service. Take notes while the sermon is being delivered.

During times of invitation be prayerful and help when others come down for prayer or when they have responded to receive Christ. Basically, when someone responds during the invitation, the Holy Spirit has drawn them based on the preached Word of God. Most invitations are given in the following categories.

- To receive Christ through salvation
- To recommit one's life to Christ
- To prayer for some need

Some churches add additional categories for those who are Christians but desire to change membership. They are invited to join by:

- Christian experience: one that has already experienced salvation.
- Letter: One who is coming from another church with a letter of recommendation.
- Baptism in some churches allow children to "join church" and then hold classes to explain salvation more fully.

The following steps should be carried out by those receiving persons who have responded to the invitation:

1. Approach them and introduce yourself
2. Tell them you are glad they responded to the invitation
3. Discern the reason they have come down by asking probing questions such as:
   - What is God dealing with you about today?
   - What invitation are you responding to today? Regardless of the response, the next question should always be a question to determine where they are spiritually.
   - Are you sure where you will spend eternity?
   - Have you accepted Jesus Christ as your personal savior, or something similar? From this point if they have not received Christ ask if they would be willing to accept Christ as their personal savior, share the plan of salvation, and pray with them to receive Christ. Further explanation in the area of salvation can be obtained by reading additional materials on the gospel and how to present it .Some resources are evangelism materials by your denomination or church or other publications by the Joshua Ministry.
4. End with a time of prayer.

Pulpit Conduct

When ministers stand before the congregation, they stand before the people and before God. The functions carried out by ministers should always focus on God, not on the minister. Remember, ministers stand between God and the people. You stand as a representative of God. Through worship, ministers connect people to God. With this in mind, there are several things we should do and not do.

First, we should never bring attention to ourselves by the way we dress or perform our duties. Modest and non-revealing apparel is the order of the day. Secondly, whatever is communicated openly or whatever service is performed should glorify God and edify the church, its members, staff, and leadership. Thirdly, we should be attentive and supportive to others leading, communicating information, praying, or ministering the Word of God. Fourth, depending on the church, but certainly when visiting a church, one should not enter the pulpit before the pastor, unless invited or if it is allowed. Fifthly, when asked, only carry out what you are asked to do. If you are asked to pray, don't preach. If you are asked to pray, pray general prayers that ask for God's blessings, prayers of adoration for and to God, and intercessory prayers for others in crises. Prayer should never be personal or confession of one's specific sins. Confession of sin should always be the first item mentioned in prayer, as the congregation enters God's presence, but personal sins of the minister should not be mentioned, at least not in corporate worship.

Sermons

There are three types of sermons:

- **Expository**— An expository sermon is one in which an extended portion of Scripture is interpreted in relation to one theme or subject. The bulk of the material for the sermon is drawn directly from the passage and the outline consists of a series of progressive ideas centered on that one main idea.

- **Textual**—A textual sermon is one in which the main points are derived from a brief portion of Scripture. The text provides the theme of the sermon. The minor points can come from other passages.

- **Topical**—A topical sermon is one in which the main points are derived from a topic supported by multiple passages of scripture.

Preaching

The only advice I would like to give relative to preaching is, be yourself. There is nothing wrong with admiring or desiring to be able to preach like someone. However, I find it interesting that in most cases we covet style and voice projection, and not anointing or Scriptural depth. You are most anointed when you are yourself. Secondly, for best results, spend time in prayer, study, and meditation on the text. Thirdly, Never preach to generate an emotional response from the people. Sadly it is increasingly common for more people to leave worship being touched emotionally rather than fed or delivered spiritually. If you spend time with God, the power of His Word alone will generate a response. Your aim must be to preach to feed the inner man, not the flesh. God can get more done by His Spirit than what we can do with our flesh. So, be yourself and prepare spiritually.

Who Are You Serving Under?

Who are you serving under, Pastor Moses or Pastor Saul? What will they allow? Have you ever asked yourself those questions? Have you considered what kind of leadership style your pastor has—Moses or Saul? If so, this session could prove to be very insightful for you.

I believe that in order to eliminate contention in a relationship, the persons in the relationship need to know each other by their spirit and physical make up. For example, teachers can be perceived as people who think they know a lot of information. When talking to a teacher, have you ever wondered why you were given so much information, when you only asked a simple question? It's because that person is a teacher. That's what teachers do—they give information. By understanding your pastor—his or her personality and leadership style—you will be able to keep your mind clear of evil thoughts against your pastor and maintain unity in your relationship. Yes, the thoughts will come. "What did the pastor mean by that comment? Why does the pastor use another associate and not me? The Pastor did or did not... Well, you fill in the blank.

Sometimes the pastor is a Moses, and other times the pastor is a Saul. If you understand your pastor's leadership style and personality, you will better understand the decisions he or she makes and his or her comments.

Serving Under Pastor Saul

What is it like serving under a Moses or a Saul? Have you ever considered what it would be like to serve under a pastor who acts like Saul? My wife suggested that I consider David and Saul's relationship as pastor and associate. As one looks at the situations David went through, that perspective proves revealing.

David's preparation began in a field tending sheep. It was through David's field experience that God drew, anointed, and prepared him for leadership. Even before David came to the palace, he used his gifts and went through circumstances that developed him to be king. Samuel had already anointed him and called him "God's anointed." One day, Saul saw David in action as he fought against the enemy of Israel, exhibiting more faith than any soldier under Saul's leadership. Being troubled by an evil spirit, Saul heard of David's gift to play music and invited him to the palace to play and comfort him. Notice That David's gift opened the door for him and placed him in the palace where God would later raise him up as king.

David's problems (the associate) did not occur until he received more praise than Saul (the pastor). Saul was insecure in who he was and in the position in which God had placed him. From the time David was praised for killing 10, 000 and Saul was praised for kill 1,000, Saul set out to kill him. Many years of productive kingdom building was lost as Saul sought to destroy the gift that God had sent him in David. The gifts in David could undoubtedly have helped prosper the kingdom. What could have been accomplished if Saul had released the ministry gift in David? Saul was so full of jealousy that his focus on his own gifts and ministry were lost. He then existed only to kill the gifts and ministry in David. He even killed others who showed kindness toward David. Saul even tried to take the life of his own son. As associates, we do not need to look at what Saul did to David as his leader and pastor, but at David's response to Saul as his associate.

David exemplified great character and restraint when his flesh and others coached him to act in an ungodly way toward leadership. David never ran around telling others what was going on between him and Saul. In fact, the only persons he discussed the matter with were the priest (his spiritual authority), his wife (Saul's daughter), and Jonathan (Saul's son). David sought help to determine how Saul would respond toward him. He did not tell others so they could gossip about it. He never exposed Saul before the people. David never spoke an evil word toward Saul or about Saul. David never lifted his hands at Saul, though he had every reason and the opportunity to do so. David ran from Saul even though he was right. He never defended himself but allowed God to defend him. God did so, and Saul had to confess that David was a righteous man. For Saul however, one can only imagine how much he could have accomplished if he had completed God's assignment for his life.

Serving Under Pastor Moses

Moses, above all biblical characters, stands out as the one under whom most associates would love to serve. Moses unlike Saul, was secure in who he was and his ability as a leader. He exemplified the character of God and demonstrated a dependence on faith in God. When circumstances came to challenge the congregation in the desert, Moses left others in charge so that he could pray and seek God's direction for the people. He was prepared, having spent eighty years in training to lead God's people. Moses could have let his calling and years of experience fill him with pride. Yet, when his father-in-law, Jethro, suggested he place men in key positions to hear and judge matters, he did so.

Pride did not stop him from receiving good, sound wisdom, nor did he feel, as some of us do, that he had all of the answers. He did not hesitate to delegate an assignment or authority.

When it came to Joshua, Moses' associate minister, Moses released him to spy the land and to lead military campaigns. It was Moses who presented Joshua to the congregation of Israel to be the next leader after his death. I believe that it was a direct result of Moses' leadership style, that we do not find Joshua undermining Moses' leadership, or trying to form his own congregation out of the people God had given Moses to pastor. Joshua was faithful to Moses even when Moses spent long periods of time away from the people. Joshua knew where the lines of authority were drawn. Joshua never crossed those lines or challenged them.

What Will Pastor Moses and Pastor Saul Allow?

One of the most critical areas in the role of associate minister is determining what one can and cannot do. What subjects can the associate preach and teach about without encountering problems? How does the associate handle the affairs or operation of the church when the pastor or others in leadership positions are not around? What areas of counseling should the associate handle or refer to another counselor? This becomes very critical and can have long lasting adverse effects on the members and on the relationship between the pastor and the associate minister. Moses would answer these questions differently than Saul. Each church and pastor may have guidelines, which should be known, understood, and followed by the associate minister.

Do you remember the story of when King Saul became impatient waiting for Samuel the priest to return and offered a sacrifice to God? Saul obeyed the voice of the people, who were afraid of the enemy. The problem was Saul was not a priest. He was a king and a prophet, but not a priest. Samuel was both prophet and priest. Saul had acted as king, priest, and prophet—the office that was reserved only for Jesus Christ.

When Samuel returned, he asked Saul what he had done. Saul told Samuel he offered the sacrifice because he had not returned yet, and the people were crying out and needed to know whether or not they should go to battle. Samuel's replied, "Thou hast done a foolish thing. God would have established your kingdom but now he has taken the kingdom from you and given it to another." Saul went beyond his line of authority and functioned in an office that was not his calling.

There are certain subjects that an associate minister should not teach or preach while attending his church, unless approved by the pastor. I remember I was asked to teach something at a church once, but it was something that I felt in my spirit the pastor should teach. Instead of teaching the lesson, I went to the pastor and explained that I was asked to teach this subject, and I thought that I should consult with him first. The pastor thanked me and asked me not to teach the subject at that time. I am talking about subjects dealing with doctrine or controversial topics. The only exception is when the pastor gives the associate approval to teach them.

Second; associates should be careful how they inform the decision-making and affairs of the church. To put yourself in the role of the pastor and make decisions without having been given the authority to do so places you in a position where God will say, "you have done a "foolish thing." If the associates teach anything they want or make decisions beyond their given authority, their days are going to be bumpy.

How do associates handle matters of counseling? Are associates free to handle all types of counseling sessions? Should associates share any or all information with the pastor? I have been in counseling sessions where I've told the person being counseled that what they've shared with me was something that I needed to share with the pastor. As I stated above, the pastor watches out for the souls of the members and has to give an account to God. People will come to you as an associate so you will hear and advise them on something they do not want to tell the pastor. When the associate deals with others who are in a position of authority in your local church in areas of adultery, fornication, or abuse, the pastor needs to know. In some cases, notification to civil authorities is required as well.

As an associate minister, you should ask God to help you understand where lines of authority exist. Never commit your pastor or the church to do anything without first getting pastoral approval. As you work closely with the pastor and learn how the church operates, it may be permissible to make some general decisions. Once again, the amount of freedom you have in these areas will depend on the person under whom you are serving.

Questions

1. Why is it important to know the leadership style of your pastor?

_____

_____

_____

_____

2. What was Saul trying to kill when he attempted to kill David?

_____

_____

_____

_____

3. What are the benefits of the pastor and associate working together?

_____

_____

_____

_____

4. What are the results when the pastor and associates do not work together?

_____

_____

_____

_____

5. Where are the lines of authority drawn at your church?

_____

_____

_____

_____

Are you

a
Servant Leader?

Covering Weakness in Leadership

The only perfect person is Jesus. When the associate minister begins to work in the church alongside the pastor, he or she will see the flaws of the church and the humanity of the pastor. What is seen on Sunday morning in the pulpit is a human vessel being used by God. It is God using humanity to meet the needs of His people. This humanity is subject to error, and will sometimes manifest itself in an ugly manner. A preacher once told me "Never be surprised at what the flesh will do." Do not be surprised when you see the pastor or other leaders act in a non-Christian manner. You make mistakes too, don't you? You're no different than them. In fact, the only difference between the pastor and the associate minister is the office in which each are called to serve. Other than that, they are just alike and prone to sin.

One of the problems is that even though we are to walk in the Word, in character and integrity, people seem to forget that the pastor is also human and subject to shortcomings. Christendom seems to believe that ministers are God incarnate. However, the same temptations that are common to all men are also common to the pastor. In fact, I think the devil shoots larger darts at pastors than associate ministers. Yet, when the pastor falls short, we are prone to uncover rather than cover the fault.

The Bible calls one who goes around revealing things about someone a talebearer (Proverbs 11:13). Are you a talebearer? Do you talk negatively behind the back of the pastor? Do you tell others what the pastor said that you don't like? Do you talk about the pastor? Are you critical about the decisions that the pastor makes? Do you reveal the pastor's shortcomings? As associate ministers, we are to cover the faults and shortcomings of others. *"Brethren, if a man be overtaken in a fault, ye which are spiritual, restore such a one in the spirit of meekness; considering thyself, lest thou also be tempted" (Galatians 6:1).* I am not talking about sin, but faults. If there is a sin it should be handled by those to whom the pastor is held accountable, those who are over the pastor in the Lord, and not by the associate minister. Associates should not gossip about the sin, but cover the pastor in prayer.

In Genesis 9, Ham got in trouble when he exposed the fault of his father, his spiritual authority, instead of covering it. He was a talebearer running around telling others about his father's fault. The Bible is clear in the Galatians passage above: If we do not cover the faults of others, the same thing can happen to us. We must cover through prayer and silence the faults of those in leadership, as well as others.

We also need to be careful about what we say about the pastor's spouse. Sometimes associates hold pastors in high esteem, but not his or her mates. You cannot respect the pastor if you do not respect the spouse of the pastor. If you talk about the pastor's spouse, you will reap what you sow and receive the judgment of God too. Remember Aaron and Miriam, Moses' brother and sister? They both spoke against Moses because he married an Ethiopian woman and because they felt that God could speak to them as well as Moses. Miriam was struck with leprosy. The Scripture does not indicate that God executed judgment against Aaron. However, the point is that God brought judgment against someone for speaking against leadership. The Scriptures warn us against touching God's anointed (1 Chronicles 16:22, Psalm 105:15). This means physically or verbally. Our role as associates should be taken seriously. It is dangerous when we talk about leadership rather than cover their faults.

Several years ago, some men burned down a Christian camp for inner city youth. These men were racists and did not want the camp to succeed. Four of these men died violent deaths. The fifth man apologized for his sin and, as far as I know, did not die violently. I also know a lady with whom I attended church several years ago who shared that she had talked about the pastor. Her home began to fall apart and mildew began to grow on the walls. Her life began to unravel before her. She knew that this was a direct result of her talking about her pastor rather than praying about the situation. Talking about the pastor or doing things against the ministry or vision of God are critical issues. What goes around comes around. The Book of Galatians calls it sowing and reaping.

The principle of sowing and reaping has its origin in Genesis 8:22. The Scripture states that *"While the earth remaineth seedtime and harvest, and cold and heat, and summer and winter, and day and night shall not cease (Genesis 8:22)."* So, in the beginning, God established this principle and there is no way around it. In the Book of Galatians, Paul says it this way: *"Be not deceived; God is not mocked: for whatsoever a man soweth, that shall he also reap" (Galatians 6:7)*. This principle suggests that whatever we do is going to come back to us. This should cause all of us to walk circumspectly and with godly fear. If you are faithful in your current ministry, you will reap what you have sown. God will send faithful people to your ministry. If you support your pastor, God will send someone to support you. If you commit yourself, someone will commit to your ministry. If you point the people to the pastor, you will reap people who point the members of your church to you. If you cover the faults of your pastor, you will have associate ministers who will cover you. However, if you talk about the pastor, someone is going to talk about you. If you expose the faults of your pastor, someone will expose your faults. If you are not faithful you will have unfaithful people in your ministry. If you leave the church prematurely, your associates will leave before their time, and you will reap the results becoming overworked, overwhelmed, and burned out. Whatever you are doing and not doing, you will reap in your people. Don't preach faithfulness to your congregation if you were not faithful to your pastor. Repent first, and then you can preach it. If possible, along with repentance, go back and ask your former pastor to forgive you. Don't expect your people to treat you like some kind of a god when you gave your pastor hell. You want people to support your vision, and yet, you wouldn't support the vision of your pastor. Don't expect what you have not sown! If you do not feel that you can support your pastor and the vision of the church, move on.

If things are being done that compromise God's Word, harm members, or are immoral, they should be covered in prayer and then discussed and handled with the proper leadership. I know we are human, and we talk about things. However, if we do, we should talk in general terms as much as possible and seek to not destroy other's character with our tongues. If our motive is to expose, tear down, or expose sin, our motives are not right. Everything we do and say should be done with a redemptive motive in mind. I am not saying we should allow sin or things that are not right to continue without correcting them. I am saying it should be done with prayer, following biblical principles, handle problems within proper leadership, in church rules and bylaws with the purpose of restoration.

Some never try to restore, they just get mad and leave. There are a number of well-meaning persons who have gone out and started churches, but they left the wrong way. They wonder why they are catching it at every hand. They ask themselves, "Why does it seem like God has gone on a vacation? Why is there no growth in the church? Why can't I ever get anyone to support me?" Maybe the answer lies in the principle of sowing and reaping. Maybe they are reaping what they have sown somewhere else.

We must always consider what we do and how we do it. What we do must always be done within the context of biblical principles giving glory to God, promoting His kingdom, and serving people. Remember, we are always being watched by God and others.

Restoring Fallen Leaders - What do we do with the Leper?

Our role as a body of believers is to represent Christ to the entire world. Although pastors and associates are church leaders, they are human and no less a part of the world. They may at times disappoint us by their language, choices, or behavior. Problem resolution is a day to day dynamic of church life and its practice results in improved relationships, and processes.

However, the impact of a pastor or associate's actions, choices or behavior is sometimes so severe that their personal integrity, witness, relationship with church membership or community is damaged. When that occurs their ability to serve is compromised. The leader has therefore "fallen" in standing. The high standard of being a Godly leader is not met.

Yet in reflecting the very character of Christ to the world, believers are to exam how we represent Christ in contending with and restoring fallen leaders back to fellowship with God. In the Old Testament people often treated fallen leaders as lepers (Leviticus 13:44). They were placed out of the camp and in the event they came near other people would have to cry "unclean, unclean." I believe we can begin examining a more effective, Godly approach to ministering to the fallen associate or pastor by starting a dialog on the subject. Our direction should ultimately be leading the fallen associate or pastor back to fellowship with God and also healing the hurting church. Let me suggest the following as thoughts to stimulate dialog.

1. Rather than labeling the fallen associate or pastor as "damaged goods" how can we demonstrate that we are instruments of God's restoring grace and love by restoring them to a place of usefulness in Christ's church.

2. Are there any sins which disqualify a fallen leader from ministering or pastoring once they have fallen?

3. Are we to ever banish an associate or pastor to a life absent of all ecclesiastical service?

4. Is there a more appropriate environment for a fallen pastor to experience the restoring power of God's grace than among the people he sinned against?

5. What is meant by, "spiritual leaders restore those whom have fallen?" (Galations 6:1)

6. How should the biblical act of casting lots found in Acts 2, and The Holy Spirit's directing in Acts 13, guide us when repented leaders are returned to a leadership position?

7. What principles from the following scriptures can we learn regarding how we handle persons who have fallen? John 8:1-11; 2 Samuel 11-12; Mark 14: 66-72

8. What is the process for restoring fallen leaders? In context with Galatians 6:1, 2 discuss the words; fault, spiritual, restore, meekness, as well as what it means to bear one's burden.

9. Remembering the cities of refuge (Numbers 35:9–34 and Johsua 20: 1–9) should we send fallen pastors to a another church or ministry during the restoration process?

10. What takes place after the pastor's public repentance is at least as important as before their disclosure.

11. Should a fallen leader assume the same position from which they fell?

12. What specific track should be established to follow those leaders that have fallen. Is that track biblically based?

Associate's Introspection

As you reflect on the content of this lesson, ask 'What is God saying to me?" Is there something in word or deed for which you need to ask forgiveness? After asking God's forgiveness, what course of action will you take to prevent the same occurrence? At this time reflect, and then use the space below to record your course of action.

1. What God is saying?

_____

_____

_____

_____

_____

_____

2. My course of action is:

_____

_____

_____

_____

_____

_____

   Father, forgive me for the sin or sins I have committed. My sin is against you and Heaven. I ask you to help me to not _____ again, but do those things that will promote unity and bring glory to your name. In Jesus' name, Amen.

   My prayer is that you will apply what has been prayerfully conveyed through the pages of this manual. I pray you will become the associate minister who reflects God's character and labor in you.

Other Resources by Dr. David Hopewell Sr.

BOOKS

The Joshua Ministry, an evangelical strategy based in principle on the Book of Joshua

Keys to Becoming an Effective Associate Minister & Church Leader

Joshua Implementation Manual

Unity, The Highest Form of Evangelism

Set the Captives Free

Joshua Ministry School of Evangelism Training Manual

SCHOOLS

The Joshua Ministry School of Evangelism

The Joshua Ministry School of Associate Minister Training
Online Courses Available

ADDITIONAL INFORMATION

www.joshuaministry.com
Email: dhopewellsr@joshuaministry.net

ADDITIONAL NOTES

ADDITIONAL NOTES

ADDITIONAL NOTES

_____

_____

_____

_____

_____

_____

_____

_____

_____

_____

_____

_____

The Joshua Ministry
www.joshuaministry.com
Email: dhopewellsr@joshuaministry.net